L. D Luke

A Journey from the Atlantic to the Pacific Coast by Way of Salt Lake City

L. D Luke

A Journey from the Atlantic to the Pacific Coast by Way of Salt Lake City

ISBN/EAN: 9783744753845

Printed in Europe, USA, Canada, Australia, Japan

Cover: Foto ©Andreas Hilbeck / pixelio.de

More available books at **www.hansebooks.com**

A JOURNEY

FROM THE

ATLANTIC TO THE PACIFIC COAST

BY WAY OF

SALT LAKE CITY

RETURNING BY WAY OF

THE SOUTHERN ROUTE,

DESCRIBING THE NATURAL AND ARTIFICIAL SCENES OF BOTH LINES.

BY

L. D. LUKE.

PRICE, 25 CENTS.

UTICA, N. Y.
ELLIS H. ROBERTS & CO., BOOK AND JOB PRINTERS.
1884.

A JOURNEY FROM THE ATLANTIC TO THE PACIFIC COAST.

An account of New York alone would furnish sufficient matter to fill a volume, but as all my readers are conversant with its history, I pass along through this rich and fertile State, and make no stop until arriving at Utica, where I purchased a first class unlimited ticket to San Francisco, California, for $129.39, September 17th, 1883. At 6.40 P. M., I took the cars on the New York Central, and crossed the bridge at Buffalo into Canada at 1 A. M. Tuesday morning, and arrived at St. Thomas on the Canada Southern Railroad at daylight.

This country is not inviting, the land is low and wet, and no good buildings are seen. It is well timbered with elm, ash, and sycamore. It produces wheat, oats, and grass. Before reaching Detroit the Custom Officer stamped our baggage. The cars were run on to a boat and ferried across to the city at 10 A. M.,—261 miles from Buffalo.

I can not pass this city, so rich in ancient lore, without a few remarks. It was visited in the sixteenth century. In 1701 Fort Ponchartrain was built by the French, who held the territory fifty-nine years, until 1760, when it was transferred to the English. In 1796 it was ceded to the United States, and incorporated as a town in 1802, and burned in 1805. In the war of 1812 it was again taken by the English, who held it one year. It received its first city charter in 1815, and was the residence of General Grant from 1846 to 1850. Located as it is on the route of all vessels to the upper lakes, and its railroad facilities, it has become a rich, flourishing and popular city, of 125,000 inhabitants, which double in every decade.

Its manufactures are various, among which we notice cars, pins, matches, organs, stoves, shoes, safes, &c. Its streets are regularly laid out, wide and airy.

The buildings are extremely fine, among which we notice the City Hall, 90 by 120 feet on the ground, and 200 feet high; containing the largest clock in the world save one. The building and grounds cost $600,000.

The Opera House, Merchants' Exchange, Odd Fellows' Hall, High School, and Public Library, are all large, costly edifices. The Library contains 40,000 volumes for public beneficence. The city supports many benevolent institutions also.

I received the hospitality of Brother Lorenzo Sellick, and tarried till the next day, Wednesday, 19th, at 10 A. M. I then left Detroit on the Michigan Central Railroad—in Michigan. From here to Upsilanti, thirty miles, is a beautiful farming country. Farther on we passed through Kalamazoo, of 12,000 inhabitants, which lies in a good farming country also.

4

After passing the high bridge at Niles, we soon came to Michigan City, near the lake—that great lumber market—arriving at Chicago at 8 P. M., 540 miles west of Buffalo. The conductor gave me a pass to the Union Depot, which the baggage master exchanged for an omnibus ticket that carried me to the wrong station. Changing to another 'bus I was soon at the right point, where a man, showing his badge, said, "I will conduct you to the right car, that is my business."

Yet, to my surprise, he led me directly across the street, and offered me a seat at the supper table first. Kindly thanking him for his benevolence, I sought my own car.

Since the fire Chicago has been rebuilt in a more beautiful and substantial manner than before.

I left the city at 10 o'clock in the evening, and passed over most of the level, rich and fertile prairie lands of the State of Illinois in the night, on the Chicago, Burlington and Quincy Railroad.

At 7 o'clock Thursday morning, September 20th, we crossed over the Mississippi River on a long iron bridge at Burlington into Southern Iowa—752 miles from Buffalo.

We soon passed on again over the rich productive prairies, that seem to have no end, and crossed the Des Moines River at Ottumwa, yet on, and still on to Creston, the end of the division—942 miles west of Buffalo. From Creston to the western bounds of the State the country is not much settled, and grass covered prairie continues all the way. The rich soil of Iowa produces all the cereals, grains, vegetables, and roots, in great abundance, common to the Temperate Zone and many of the fruits. Wood is scarce, but coal is abundant.

It is mined to a great extent at Tyrone, and new mines are being opened at Russell, at a depth from 150 to 300 feet, with strata from 3 to 7 feet.

Those at Lucas, in Lucas County, are the best in the State. Waste coal by the way-side was burning by spontaneous combustion at the Cleveland mines.

The first timber discovered was on the valley of the Missouri River, and that very scattering, and of a stinted growth. The valley is from five to ten miles wide, and places are crowned with high bluffs.

The Platte River forms a junction with the Missouri River at Plattsmouth, where we crossed the long steel bridge, 852 miles from Buffalo, connecting the State of Iowa with the State of Nebraska. It comprises two span, 480 feet each, approached by a trestle three-quarters of a mile long, and cost more than a million of dollars.

I put up at the Perkins House, Plattsmouth, Nebraska. The town has the railroad shops, and nestles in a little valley.

From the cliffs above is an extensive view of the surroundings. Leaving Plattsmouth Friday, September 21st, on the Burlington and Missouri River Railroad, in Nebraska, known as the Great Burlington Route. Our course followed the valley of the Platte, twenty-five miles to Ashland, where we struck the South Fork, then turning southwest, and followed up the valley of that river fifty miles to Lincoln, the capital of the State, where eight lines of railroads form a junction. All the extravagant stories that have been told of the richness, fertility and beauty of the farming lands in the Platte Valley have not been exaggerated. Truly, indeed, one must really see them to appreciate their loveliness and worth. No young man going west for land should stop short of Nebraska. Although all the cereals and vegetables are raised, yet corn is king. Field after field stretch on along our line, and seem to have no end, while in the distant horizon the open prairie rolls away, inviting new industry to till the soil. I was told that when the lands were once broken, a team of six horses with a screw pulverizer would fit fifteen acres in one day, being followed by a wood drag, it was ready for the seed. One team would easily plant fifteen acres per day. Fifty bushels is a day's work husking; it is put into cribs holding from six to 750 bushels each; 5,000 bushels in one year on a farm of 120 acres is no uncommon yield. From six to eight horses are used on the shellers, which shell it off as fast as two men can shovel in, stripping off from 1,400 to 1,500 bushels per day. They have no fences—the stock is herded by cow boys, who have one dollar per head during the season.

Lincoln is a railroad centre, where five lines meet, a smart little town, having the finest post office west of the Mississippi River, built of cut stone. From Lincoln we kept our southwest course twenty miles, until we crossed the Big Blue River, then took a direct west course eighty miles, across an uninhabited, open prairie—one vast ocean of grass, in all its primeval loneliness—until we reached Hastings, another railroad centre, standing in the midst of surrounding solitude. At Hastings we turned at right angle, and went south thirty miles; struck the Republican River at Red Cloud, and took supper there.

At that point we turned our course directly west, following the valley of that river the remaining part of the night. At daylight Saturday morning, September 22d, we crossed the line into the State of Colorado.

Nothing near us could be seen except one broad expanse of prairie, rolling away in its blank nakedness for hundreds of miles without a tree, plant, or shrub, or any thing to break the monotony of the scene; until the expanse sinks beneath the horizon, on the peaks of the far distant Colorado mountains. We have passed the rich soil of the Platte, and here we find it scarcely four inches deep, underlaid with a white sand, and coated over with a mat of buffalo grass, about four inches high, which is dried down to hay, having a brown and crisp appearance, yet it is said that stock and buffalos feed and thrive upon it. Some, however, must have died from some cause, as the only products to be seen along the whole route for shipment, is a few piles of buffalo bones.

We took breakfast at Akron, which is merely an eating house to accommodate travel.

After starting along again, all eyes were set on the distant peaks of the Rocky Mountains. As we drew nearer, they appeared to rise higher and more high, until they stood in mighty grandeur before us.

We reached the city of Denver at 11 A. M., 1,671 miles west of Buffalo. Nothing could be more astonishing to [me than after traveling for hundreds of miles across an open, wild, and uninhabited prairie, to be at once ushered into a rich and populous city of 70,000 inhabitants; where wealth, opulence and grandeur meet. The public buildings are trimmed with cut stone of bright colors and different hues; representing a great degree of artistic beauty.

The Opera House is very tastefully trimmed, and cost over a million of dollars, and it is said to be the finest house of the kind in the United States. The depot is built of cut stone at a cost of $600,000. The City Hall is built of cut stone also, of three different colors, very rich and ornamented; cost $310,000.

The town is laid out in squares, set with cotton wood trees, and water from the mountains and 20 flowing artesian wells, distributed, flows down all its streets. The water from the wells which are from 300 to 400 feet deep, is very clear and pure, but not cold; affording a good supply.

The private buildings are tastefully erected, from three to five stories high, composed of wood, iron and stone. The shops are supplied with every article of convenience on the globe. Their telegraph poles are two feet through, spliced, and 60 feet high, ascended by iron steps driven in the sides and carry 160 wires.

We have now passed the beautiful prairied west, so much admired, so much extolled in song, where peaceful rivers gently wind their way through fields of golden grain; as well as the untold millions of acres of land that still lies in its native wildness, where nature's plastic hand first gave it form. All is left behind, while before us the Rocky Mountains rise up in bold affront and seem to defy our farther progress. Before leaving the city I inquired from whence they gained so much wealth. The answer from all was the same. It comes from the rich mines in the mountains that surround us.

Four railroads diverge from here. At 7:15 P. M. I took the Denver and Rio Grande railroad that led directly south along the irregular contour of the Rocky Mountain range 75 miles to Colorado Springs. As the road climbed steadily upwards, the snow capped peaks became more and more visible, stretching away to the south and west in the hazy distance, until the outlines were lost in the horizon, but Pike's Peak stood directly before us, clothed in white, ready for retirement as the day was fast drawing to a close.

Colorado Springs was founded in 1871 and now contains 6,000 inhabitants. The streets are lined with trees, and water courses passing through them. The business houses are large, and it has one of the finest opera houses in the country. "The Antlers," a new and spacious hotel, costing over $150,000, takes the place of the little log cabin which once served as a hostelry. In the town are churches of every denomination. It must be remembered that there are no springs at this place, they are located in Manitou, at the foot of Pike's Peak, on a branch road five miles distant, which I took, arriving at 10 P. M., and put up at the Bell House.

Manitou nestles in a narrow valley, being shut in on three sides by the foot hills of the Rockies. Its only importance is a watering place for invalids, and a resort for tourists and pleasure seekers, in search of the wild and sublime beauties of nature. It is well provided with public houses, some of which are very large and commodious. It also has a new and splendid bath house, and all the conveniences for the comfort and happiness of invalids. It has a population of 500 which is rapidly increasing. No other watering place on the globe has so many wild attractions, sublime and soul-stirring scenes, that strike the mind with such wonder and reverential awe—lying in close proximity—as Manitou.

Pike's Peak, the Cave of Stalactites, Williams Canon, Rainbow Fall, Red Canon, Garden of the Gods, Glen Eyrie, Devil's Punch Bowl, Cheyenne Canon and Manitou Park. Then to cap the grandeur of all, to stand upon some cloud-capped eminence and look off in space, and see the different peaks of the mountains shooting up fantastically in every conceivable shape and form, like an ocean in its wildest gambols, ruffled by a stormy tempest.

The medical springs located at Manitou are six in number. The Navajoe, from which water supplies the bath house; also the Iron, Ute, the Sulphur, the Maniton, Ute-Soda and Little Chief. The water is said to be palatable to those accustomed to it, but to me it was most loathsome.

————

September 23d was the Sabbath. Still remembering that Christ went up into a mountain to pray, I took a lunch and started for that lone retreat, to spend the day in seclusion with nature and my God alone. I started up a canon clothed with verdure, and a torrent stream foaming and rushing headlong down its course. On my right and left the granite walls rose thousands of feet above my head, on top of which two mighty figures stand in human form, called Gog and Magog. Many little grottoes were seen far up the inaccessible cliffs where human foot has never trod. Innumerable masses of rock stand out in open relief far up the dizzy heights above, resembling various objects of reality: such as giants, fortifications, and the like. One represents a steamboat with smoke-stack and boiler. A few miles up I passed a side canon, yet still I wound around onward and upward, among immense fallen masses of rock that were piled up one upon the other in wild confusion in the canon below, while through the masses the torrent stream dashing, foamed and spent its fury. Still to the right and left the cliffs rise up and seem to pierce the clouds.

Hemmed in a narrow defile, an awful chasm, following up a burro trail a foot wide, I found myself on the highway to Pike's Peak. Turning to the right and crossing the gulch on a rude bridge to the other side, I discovered Sheltered Falls rushing out from under the fallen masses of rock, rolling and foaming in its headlong course down the rocky abyss. While down here below, I could not keep my eyes off from the many objects on the towering heights above. I saw in form a mighty railroad car roofed out 100 feet, a noble gothic cottage, a king's crown, and an extensive cemetery with its numerous monuments rising high in air amid the scattered verdure with which its surface was overgrown. Paralyzed I stood and gazed in wondrous thought, my vision beheld it, my imagination grasps it, my tongue can't explain it, my pen can't portray it. The mighty works of God. Anon crossing and recrossing this torrent, I at length came to a wooded section of tall pines, on a descending plateau. While passing through this I heard the low growling of a cat; I looked, and behold in a crouching form the animal was approaching me. I drew my revolver and assumed an attitude of defence; but giving a sudden scatt! I was again left in silent blessedness. Emerging from this grove and passing a little cascade, I again came out into open view of "peaks that o'er peaks appeared, and seemed to reach the sky, but when they were trod, far on beyond, new cliffs o'er cliffs, arose." Many of which had been burned over, and nothing but utter barren, naked rock appeared. Toiling up the steep ascent in the hot sun, with perspiration on my brow, I looked up and saw the snow clad summit of Pike's Peak. O, how refreshing the sight; how soon I thought to be there, and view the surroundings; then return to my hotel. Little dreaming that I was yet six or eight miles away, with the steepest part of the grade to climb yet, and the toil, suffering and fatigue I must endure to reach that point. To see summer and eternal winter, apparently clasp hands was a novel sight.

But O, how deceitful is distance in climbing a mountain. Altitude appears to annihilate space. I had now left the mountain stream behind, while heat and perspiration increased my thirst. Looking down a mile below I saw a little lake where placid waters lay, and mocked my thirst. O, cruel fate that hath denied that cooling draught to wet my parched lips. It is Lake Moraine; covers 40 acres, and is 60 feet deep, clear and cold. Its altitude is over 10,000 feet.

Winding and turning in the ascent I soon began to feel a cooling atmosphere, and on arriving at the line where vegetation ceases to grow, I came to a spring that was frozen, and the water and mud about it was held in icy chains.

I looked up above and about me, and nothing could be seen but masses of broken rocks, shivered and splintered to pieces, and hurled down from the heights above, and piled upon each other in the rudest form, and chaotic confusion was seen everywhere. I trembled at the sight, and adored a Creative Power.

The sun had now sunk beneath the horizon. My limbs grew weary, my heart beat audibly in the rarified atmosphere. The chills of evening were gathering around me, and patches of snow were under my feet. Should I return, it was ten miles back. Should I proceed, it was three miles to the summit, and no moon to shine upon the narrow trail through which I must pick my way. Resolving to proceed, I picked up a couple of coffee sacks, rolled them around my hands as a sort of muff, and slowly plodded along.

From weariness I sat down upon every friendly rock I came to, for rest and breath. The mountain breeze chilled me through, and I shook like an aspen leaf. Every few rods, instead of sitting I would lay down under some sheltering rock for rest, breath, and protection from the wind. The trail now became slippery, and the broken fragments of granite were covered with ice. Weary with the toils of the day, chilled with the coldness of night, trembling in every nerve my feet tripped at every obstacle, I would fall flat on my face and remain until my heart ceased to flutter and throb in a measure; then, feeling invigorated, I would arise and with new courage start on; but as soon as the motion of my feet commenced, the internal motion also commenced, and it seemed as though I had a trip-hammer within my breast, and felt a relaxation and sickness besides. I knew not what ailed me, and began to fear I might perish there on the mountain side alone, not realizing I was breathing a rarified atmosphere I had never inhaled before.

Prone on the snow and ice I poured out my supplications to the God who rules on high. A few moments on my feet, and more on the snow, I gradually arose until some time in the night I espied a little hut on top of the mountain; with joy I started for it, when I ought to have taken the right hand trail that would have led me to a better place; but I missed it in the darkness and supposed I was on the only track. Arriving at the small stone house, having two windows and a door, where I loudly rapped, and in the most piteous tones, plead for mercy and protection. I heard heavy foot-steps within, but no voice responded to mine. It was a stable, with a mule inside. I went entirely around it and looked in every direction for the abode of man. Nothing but snow could be seen, and no visible trail led from it. I was reduced to the alternative of choosing a perishing condition without, or seeking such an humble shelter within as that in which my Saviour was born. Finding a floor and two more coffee sacks, and being sheltered from the wind, I felt myself happy, and praised a Creator's name. Notwithstanding my happy condition, I could not get warm, but trembled and shook till daylight appeared, then, looking over the crest of the mountain, I discovered the low signal station covered with snow. So near where joy and happiness abound, and I knew it not. I hastened there, the signal boys got up and made me warm; gave me a cup of coffee, but I could not eat.

When the sun was well up one of the signal boys went out on top of the mountain and showed me the surrounding scenes. Looking to the east we saw Manitou at the foot of the mountain, and Colorado Springs in close proximity, also the Garden of the Gods on the left, while the broad stretching prairie rolled on until it was lost in the horizon. Then turning to the south we beheld directly before us the peaks that rise and shoot up in every conceivable shape and form, as though nature had frolicked with herself, and when in the height of her carnival was at once frozen stiff. Still beyond all this, in the far distance could be seen the Sangre De Christo that closed the view in that direction. Southwest the fantastic peaks held our attention a few moments, and then the vision extends on for hundreds of miles and rested on the snow range that is clad in perpetual winter.

On the north down the perpendicular side of the mountain is the Bottomless Pit, not of fire, but of eternal snow and ice.

The top of the mountain is oval, comprising an area of four acres, composed of nothing but broken rocks, being the highest point in the United States, and the most elevated habitation on the globe, where only two signal station boys stay a portion of the time. A marble slab stands directly on the summit, on which I read,

"Fair Cynthia with her starry train,
Shall linger o'er thy silent rest ;
And waft one soft, sweet spirit strain
To Erin, among the blest."

Erected by Serj. John and Morah O'Keef, in memory of their infant daughter, Erin O'Keef, who was destroyed by mountain rats at the U. S. Signal Station on the summit of Pike's Peak, March 25th, 1876.

No vehicle has ever ascended this mountain yet ; everything even to the wood they burn is brought up on burro trains, that is on mules' back. Returning again to the station about noon, a company on burros arrived, and a lady among the rest, who dropped at once into a chair, relaxed, and exclaimed, "O, I wish I could die !" She had my sympathy. I drank another cup of coffee, gave my host a dollar for accommodations, and started back. Having traveled a mile or two my strength failed, and I stretched myself out on a rock. Two gentlemen came along down on horseback and stopped, one dismounted, saying, "Here, my friend, get on and ride down this steep grade, and I will walk." I rode about a mile, and then returned his horse with my most grateful thanks.

After going a little farther, I looked back up the mountain, and behold, one of the signal boys was coming down on the government mule, who broke the stillness of the night by his steps on the floor, while I lay quivering in one corner as his only companion. He is one of the noblest of his kind, and I obtained his picture. The young man at once got off, saying, "Here, my dear friend, get on and ride ; I am more able to walk than thou." I felt that God had blessed me, and I highly appreciated the favor. I was surprised to see with what caution and precision the animal took every step, never stumbling or missing his foothold all the way down. We arrived at Manitou at dark. I returned the faithful animal to its owner, gave him a dollar, and my blessings also, then repaired to the Bell House.

Tuesday, September 25th, I visited the Stalactite Cave. My course led up William's Canon a mile and a quarter. The rocky sides rise from 200 to 300 feet perpendicular, and the hills above rise much higher.

It appears as though nature by one cleft of her power had split the mountain in twain, and in places there is barely room for the wagon track, while at the narrows the road seems to be closed, and the track passes under overhanging rocks, and terminates at the Bridal Veil Falls, which has a descent of seventy feet. The broken, jagged and rugged rocks high up on these precipicies represent spires, temples, towers, arches and steeples. Masonic arch is high up on the clifts. The Temple of Juno is seen on the left. The Temple of Isis is hollow, with various openings for doors and windows, and looks very natural.

The mouths of many grottoes present themselves high up on the inaccessible cliffs, and are called windows.

One of the most remarkable of all the natural scenes on earth is found in this Canon, about a mile from Manitou, where the walls slope back a little, so that by winding and turning we ascend 170 feet, and come to a cleft or crevice in the rocks running at right angle with the Canon, which is spanned by two natural bridges. Under these we pass in ascending a flight of wooden steps for the next 100 feet, which brings us to the mouth of a grotto, in which is a Temple of Nature, made by God's own hand, ornamented and embellished with the most exquisite workmanship of his power. Such as stalactites, stalagmites, alabaster, frescoed walls, musical appliances, statuary of men, animals, birds, beasts and creeping things, besides thousands of other undescribed objects.

The entrance is guarded by doors to the ante-room, where guests register; this is fifteen feet long, seven feet wide, and seven feet high. Stooping under a rock we go through a narrow path to the dressing room, eighteen by fifteen feet and ten feet high. There is a smooth surfaced rock in this room forming a natural table, on which guests lay their hats and bonnets, and are provided with dark muslin dresses, if they wish them.

Our candles being lighted, we follow a narrow path a few feet and pass under a low arch three feet thick, that is covered with stalactite material, from which we at once emerge into Cascade Hall. This room is eighteen by ten feet and fifteen feet high. In this is a large cascade of dripstone, resembling water falling over rocks, fifteen feet, and overhung with stalactites. A flight of stairs descend twenty feet to rooms below, and on the opposite side is a flight of stairs to rooms above, entered by a tunnel forty feet long, on the wall of which is the form of a man hanging by one arm, and at the end of the tunnel is a dry well, on which rests two flight of steps. Ascending one of these, we came to a long tunnel, inside of which is a foot and leg of an elephant almost perfect. Ascending another stairway, and passing through a crevice, we arrive at Canopy Hall, which is 230 feet long, 30 feet wide and 30 feet high, filled with wonders and lighted by a locomotive headlight.

In a crevice over head are hundreds of stalactites standing in line by twos and threes until darkness obscures the view.

On a projecting shelf are stalagmites resembling so many candles. Walking down over carbonate of lime into a side room, twenty feet long and sixteen feet high, brought us to the icy curtain, which is fluted and flounced in artistic style.

It contains many stalactites and mounds of clay covered a foot thick with lime formation. Still farther we passed under an arch into another part, bringing us into a spacious room, in one corner of which, the inclined rock floor, appears to be a rippling stream. In the room also were seen stalactites of such infinite number and form that my pen fails to describe them. Turning about, our steps led down to a basin which is fifteen feet across and five feet deep. Water has stood in it for untold ages. Crossing over this on a bridge, and ascending farther we pass stalactite, large and small, with fluted columns; also on a projecting rock is seen the old hog's head, with large eyes and ears and upturned nose, also the suspended columns. Leaving this room of the beautiful, and turning to the left and stooping slightly, we pass into Boston Avenue, 500 feet long, which is low, narrow and very crooked, leading to a small side room, where we ascend a flight of stairs and pass twenty feet through a small aperture called Tall Man's Misery, into the dining room, where the workmen once eat their dinner. This room has two halls leading to it and two leading from it. Its size is ten by sixteen feet and twenty feet high. Then crossing over a bridge into the Hall of Beauty, passing by the slice of bacon, the pig's ear, cave of cinders, Jacob's ladder, lake basin, skylights, furnace grate and pillow of stalactite, into Chicago Avenue, which is so narrow that visitors pass it in single file, going by the thigh and foot and clusters of flowers, into Music Hall, seventy feet long, ten feet wide and twenty feet high. Here, under a bridge, hang a large number of stalactites, which are musical, giving forth the tones of an organ.

Here are also some of the finest flowering alabaster in the cave, and the walls are incrusted with it. There are clusters of stalactites surrounded by beds of flowers, and on the side wall is seen the sleeping bird.

Another avenue leads to St. Almon's Rest, in which is the sheep's head and also a post office, where visitors leave their cards. Descending twelve feet brought us to the Old Maid's Kitchen. Going down stairs we enter Alabaster Hall, thirty feet long and five feet wide. The ceiling is oval, and every inch of space covered with alabaster flowers. They can not be described, they are as white as the driven snow and infinite in form. Cathedral Alcove, Floral Temple, &c., have untold beauties, such as translucent bunches of alabaster, coral wreaths, stalactites innumerable, and the needleization of crystalized lime is infinitely fine and tinny, and astonishes the beholder when looking upon it. Untold millions of crystalized needles are sticking out of the wall, surrounded by branches of the same material, which glitter and dazzle in the torch lights. Going a little farther we came to the last, but not the least, of these grotto wonders. The room is ten feet high, eighteen feet wide and twenty-five feet long, with the floor rising on the back side. No one approaches any farther than the doorway, which is oval at the top, five feet wide and six feet

high. Without contradiction, we say this is the finest under-
ground room in the world. The roof is hung with stalactite
icicles and stalagmites rising from the bottom. One representing
a bride adorned for the wedding, surrounded by translucent shafts,
chandeliers, candlesticks, pillars, supporting urns and vases, while
over her head the ceiling is fully covered with floral, amid the
pendant icicles with which it is sprinkled o'er. All in and around
this hall is of the purest white. The right hand side of the
chamber is called the museum, where apparently the Great Artist
wrought the plastic material into works of creation rather than
fiction, such as flowers, vegetables, beets, carrots, parsnips, birds,
snakes, and almost every conceivable form of vegetable and
animal kingdom. Its beauties can never be told; it must be seen
to be appreciated. The scientist can not describe it, and I will
attempt it no farther. The cave was discovered June 26th, 1880,
by two boys, John and George Picket. It is owned by Rinehart
and Snider, and must be a source of great wealth, as one dollar
fee is charged for entrance. Emerging from this cavern of beauty,
I ascended to the lofty heights above, and cast my eyes south on
the rocky peaks that shoot up in grand fantastic sublimity, scooped
by the same hand and formed by the same Power Divine that
caused those beauties to appear below. And how little am I,
standing between the two speechless, gazing on the sublime
grandeur in silence, when a spirit voice fell on my ear, saying, "I
am here, these works are mine." I retired in meditation. After
dinner my footsteps led me towards the Garden of the Gods, so
called because man has had nothing to do with its formation.

I had not gone far before a gentleman overtook me, riding alone
in a buggy, and asked me to ride. The first object noticed was a
mighty frog, twenty feet in length, sitting on his feet on top of a
distant rock. Then soon appeared a mighty blacksmith's anvil,
twenty feet high; then a giant's head with deep sunken eyes and
yawning mouth; next appeared the ruined city, a name I applied
because the numerous shafts of red sand stone shooting up and
overcapped by broad slabs of blue limestone, represent so many
chimneys after the buildings had been demolished. On a massive
rock lies a huge alligator that never winks.

On an eminence that overlooks the plateau beyond, stands
balance rock so poised and of such immense weight that storms
and tempest can not move it. Advancing upon the smooth surface of the plane, where there is not a spire of grass or the least
vestige of vegetation to break its monotony, we came to the gateway of the Garden of the Gods. From this smooth surface, and
on either side of the roadway, blades of red sandstone have been
thrown up from their stratas below and left standing edgewise,
rising for hundreds of feet in the air, with perpendicular sides, and
twenty or thirty feet thick. The top being jagged, it represents
spires, steeples, cathedrals and the like.

This upheavaling of nature took place at a very early period,
when this earth was shook from centre to circumference in such a
manner that no pen can describe it or imagination can conceive it.

Mountains were cleft asunder, and their massive fragments rolled down their sides or crushed to pieces, and piled up in chaotic confusion along their course. All nature demonstrates this fact, but no history can reach it, as it is prehistoric, and perhaps before the creation of man.

Returning now to my subject, and passing the gateway on the opposite side, in open relief rises the Tower of Babel for hundreds of feet, having numerous spires on top; and near by is Montezumas Cathedral of red sandstone, of a similar shape and size. Beyond this is seen the blue rocks, which shoot up in perpendicular blades to a great height, extending for miles, forming one eternal barrier to man and beast.

This is one of the most wonderful places in the world, although utter barrenness and desolation characterize every foot of the ground. But the innumerable shafts and blades, standing amid the garden, and the contrast of blue granite with red sandstone, all conspire to make the place admirable.

Proceeding onward we crossed Monument Creek, and followed up the bank a mile to General William J. Palmer's residence at Glen Eyrie, located on Monument Creek. These grounds being irrigated showed verdure and beauty. An exquisite tasty gateway of varnished cedar, a gate-house, conservatory, shaded walks and lawns make it really an oases in that desert country. Behind the residence rises the rugged, barren mountain. On the left and from the smooth surface of the low ground rise many shafts of red sandstone, apparently 200 feet high, resembling chimneys and of an equal size all the way up.

Turning around and retracing our steps, we saw high up on one of the lofty crags the eyrie, where the eagle reared its young. Following down the valley of Monument Creek, by the foot of the mountain, where nothing but utter barrenness is seen for five miles, brought us to the old town of Colorado City, an offspring of the early days of '49, when Pike's Peak was the objective point of all. It can now boast of nothing, only having been the seat of Colorado's first legislature. We drove to Manitou, and at the Bell House I rested quietly.

———

Wednesday, September 26th, I left Manitou about 8 A. M. and returned five miles on the branch road to Colorado Springs. At 11.50 I took the main line south, still following the banks of Fountain Creek, which we started on at Manitou, until we reached its junction with the Kansas and Pueblo, 40 miles distant, through a fine valley in which nothing will grow without irrigation. Pueblo is a small place, the junction of four rods, and has the railroad shops. Turning our course now northwest, we follow the rugged and awful channel of the Arkansas river for the next hundred miles or more to Salida. Starting along up the river for many miles through a narrow vale entirely barren except where irrigated, we only saw a little stinted corn, and miserable huts of willow poles, ten feet square, covered with dirt. The banks rise perpendicular on both sides, and are composed of alternate stratas of shale and light gray limestone. As the valley winds and turns they represent one connected and continuous line of fortifications; while their points shooting up in different forms and shapes, represent castles, spires, towers, chimnies, batteries, etc. The open country beyond represents nothing but utter nakedness of shale and stone.

Florence is a coal junction where immense quantities of coal arrive from Coal Creek.

The railroad banks are protected from washing by slag from the silver ores. Canon City is a little town where the Silver Cliff road makes a junction. From here the road passes through some of the grandest and most sublime scenery on earth; the Royal Gorge of the Arkansas. An open special car was run through here, on which the passengers were all seated. It moved directly into the canon where the steep sides are only moderately high, but before many minutes elapsed, we noticed they grew higher with every turn of the wheel until they seem to pierce the clouds, and rise more than one-fourth of a mile in perpendicular height; and all stand edgewise, displaying the varied colors of the rainbow. Their sides are perfectly smooth as a flag-stone from the bottom to the top, without a break in them for over 3,000 feet. There is no trees, bushes or grass clinging to them, and a bird could not find a place to rest her foot. The scene becomes darker and more dreary, and the giant walls press closer together until they approach within thirty feet of each other, and shut the sun's rays from view. Here is scarcely room for the river alone, while the track runs along on a bridge built lengthwise of the stream and suspended from steel supports mortised into the rocks overhead.

Every thing is weird, wild and strange around us, and the maddened river dashing against the rocks breaks the stillness with its awful roar.

All on board are dwarfed and dumb, beholding the power that nature possesses.

Then, on looking forward, the granite walls appeared to close and shut together, and it seemed that we must at once be crushed to pieces; but, as we approached the scene, the road gently curved and we passed around, but to see another similar feature just ahead. Thus hugging closely to the rocky walls, we wound and turned for eight miles, until we made our egress from the canon, which I have vainly tried to describe; finding letters useless and no familiar object adequate for comparison, I can only say, "how mighty are thy works, O God!"

From this point we traversed the valley of the upper Arkansas, with the serrated peaks of the Sangre de Christo close at hand on the right, until reaching the little cozy town of Salida where the Leadville branch makes a junction with the main line, a little after dark.

Holding a first class unlimited through ticket, I was here granted a free ticket to Leadville and return. The greatest mining camp in the world. About 8 P. M. I took the cars on the branch road and pursuing a northwest course, following the valley of the same river to Leadville, 125 miles from Manitou, arriving there at midnight, and at once retired.

Thursday, September 27th.—Leadville is situated in the central portion of the State of Colorado. The eastern portion of the State is one continuous unoccupied plain; while the remaining portion is covered with the Rocky Mountains, which a few years ago were considered valueless, except as the backbone to hold the continent together. But later investigation has unfolded its beauties, and developed its wealth. In scenic beauty and sublimity it rivals Switzerland; and its mineral wealth is yet untold. Inhabitants have flocked there like fowls of the air to their wonted resorts, and as by magic, it has at once been spoken into a State.

At present Leadville is the most important mining town in the State. It has a population of 20,000, and an altitude of 10,025 feet. It has no fine buildings; it boasts of no fine arts, everything is covered with dirt, and there is no reflection for a future state, and no thought but for the shining dust. Snow falls in June and July, and is never out of sight on the surrounding mountains. It was told me that no vegetables grew within 200 miles of them.

Starting out in the morning I saw trains of heavy teams coming down from the mines on the east loaded with ore for the smelters and for shipment. Casting my eyes in that direction I noticed mounds of dirt thrown out of the mining shafts scattered over the hills as far as I could see. Walking in the road that leads up California Gulch, I discovered the banks had all been washed out for gold dust.

The surface of the country is made up of broken flat stone, intermingled with brown sand and clay, and is easily carried about in the wind. Hearing a train of teams behind, I turned around and beheld a cloud of dust that enveloped the whole scene.

A little farther along I came to where three men were washing for gold. The water was caused to run down a bank of ten feet descent into a trough or spout having cleats inside holding quicksilver. The bank is then cut down, thrown into the spout, the dirt washed away into the gulch below, the stone thrown into a pile, while the quicksilver catches the particles of gold as they pass along.

While sitting here taking notes, a burly Irishman came along and unceremoniously threw some sacking into the channel, piling on stone, and turned the water off, drove the men away, disputing their claim.

Mineral is found at all depths, from the surface to 1,000 feet down. Sometimes they tunnel into the side of the mountain until they are a hundred feet below the surface, and then shaft down. Steam engines are brought into requisition to raise the mineral which is brought up in little hand cars that are dumped into a storehouse, then thrown out through shoots into wagons and drawn away. Four hundred and forty of these little car-loads are raised from one shaft in one day. One shaft is said to have a strata of from 50 to 60 feet of rock and sand mineral, 120 feet below the surface. Most of the ores are of a snuff or drab color, and a novice could not detect the mineral in them.

Silver Cord mine is 900 feet deep, has a strata of mineral 35 feet in thickness, and yields 150 tons daily, averaging 30 ounces of silver per ton.

Iron Mine is 1,100 feet on an inclined plain; but its perpendicular height is but 375 feet. The perpendicular shafts are cribbed with wood eight inches square.

Standing on the higher lands above and looking down the town has the best appearance, being surrounded by mountains entirely destitute of vegetation.

The ores are broken up in a crusher, put into a furnace and melted. The slag is drawn off into an iron bowl resting on a hand barrow, wheeled off and emptied. The metals run out into a trough and are dipped out with a ladle into dishes that forms the bars.

The Nourse Consolidated Mining and Smelting company has a capital stock of $1,000,000; 100,000 shares at $10 each.

Of the mines owned by this company we notice the Silver Plume. It has a pay streak 15 to 26 inches wide, the ore runs 40 ounces of silver and 50 or 60 per cent. of lead, 20 feet from the surface. The vein is almost perpendicular; the course of the vein is nearly north

The White Iron is decomposed iron, and ten feet wide. It runs ten ounces of silver and two ounces of gold per ton.

The Lulu has a two foot pay streak, in a five foot vein of iron, which mills 126 ounces of silver and two ounces of gold.

The Pekin has a ten foot vein which assays 170 ounces of silver.

The Kossuth has granite walls, five feet in width, yields 15 ounces of silver and 45 per cent. in copper per ton, at a depth of 15 feet.

The Dofflemeyer has returned 158 ounces of silver to the ton. The above are merely sample numbers of the whole, and the value of these mines would seem fabulous. The Nevada mine was sold in 1880 for $245,000. Silver product for 1882, was $18,000,000. Before I leave this subject I will say that miners are all compelled to furnish their own beds, and when they move from one place to another, they take up their bed and walk.

At 5 P. M. I started back for the junction at Salida; arriving there about 10. A drummer met me and escorted me across the river on the ties of the railroad bridge to a public house. As I must start before day the next morning, I paid my bill before retiring.

Friday morning, September 28.—At 4 A. M., in the darkness, I was searching my way back to the depot, which I found with some difficulty, and was soon on the main line moving west on the Denver and Rio Grande Railroad, leaving the valley of the Arkansas

B

river behind, to climb the Continental Divide, over the mountains, through Marshall's Pass, to strike the channel of the Gunnison river on the other side, which is a branch of the Rio Grande, and connects with it at Grand junction. The waters then flow on to the Colorado river.

Passing a bush grown valley, we commence to climb a moderately steep grade, but soon reach the mountains, and on looking towards the clouds, in the distance, we see a circular rim of earth and snow sheds, that marks the onward course of the road. The track doubles time and again on itself, but gradually we move upwards for a while until we arrive where the grade is very steep, the curves sharp and frequent, arduous toil is required to gain the summit, and there is no play on the programme. Two strong engines toil and pant, tugging us up the winding way through snow-sheds and tangled, half-dead forest, quivering in the snow and ice around them, thus up, up we go until we arrive at the summit of Marshall's Pass, more than two miles above the level of the sea, and one of the highest railroad points in America,—26 miles up grade from Salida, 2,185 miles from Utica, and 1,365 miles from San Francisco.

Looking back from whence we came, Mount Ouray stands at our left as a sentinel, looking down on its fellow-peaks, like a ruffled granite billow sea at its feet, rudely from the hand of nature thrown.

In the distance is the Sangre de Christo Range, white with everlasting snow.

The great San Luis Park is seen also reaching to the horizon.

Turning our face to the west, the descent is still more rapid, sharp, jagged peaks rise up from below in wild confusion, and seem to threaten immediate destruction in an awful abyss below, should we advance another step.

The fearless engine started on, and gently wound around a point, and followed a rim cut in the side of the mountain, displaying apparently a number of railroads at different points below, winding, turning, looping around, running in various directions, and seeming to have no connection with each other. Yet still a look upwards on the opposite side of a gorge would often bring to our view, the snow-sheds, we had so lately passed.

At the summit one engine, with the baggage and tender were detached and suffered to follow on behind. They were nearly all the time in sight; and always passing in an opposite direction.

Thus descending from that dizzy height, where five miles' travel scarce advanced us one, until we at length, struck the narrow vale of the Tomichi River, and followed its winding course down through the mountains until it made its egress into a wider valley below that produced a little coarse grass, the first that has been seen for over 200 miles.

From here a backward glance gives the traveler an idea of the vast heights overcome.

Then looking forward, Gunnison appears in view, where the waters of the Tomichi unites with the Gunnison River, arrivng at the town at 9 A. M.

This is the most important manufacturing and commercial City in western Colorado. It is the center of a rich gold, silver, coal, iron, and lead, mining country; and the finest steel mills in the world are being erected here, but not a specie of vegation of any kind is seen growing.

Leaving the beautiful plateau on which Gunnison is located, we at once immerged into the Black Canon, and pursue its dark and winding way for 25 miles through some of the most thrilling, awe inspiring and sublime scenery on earth.

This gorge is grander, deeper, darker, and yet more beautiful than the one we have left behind. It is thrice as long—dark hued—displaying many colors, yet cheifly composed of red sandstone, which is often broken off into shoulders as they rise, and in the crevices bushes and vines have found a footing; and hang down the darkened walls over head as a sort of green drapery, which adds much to the beauty of the scene. As we advance the cliffs grow higher and steeper, and suddenly the sunlight is shut off by the overhanging cliffs above. The gorge narrows up so much that there is scarcely room for the river and the car track, which hugs closely to the rugged walls, while the river rolls and thunders at our feet.

With a shudder, and awe inspiring feeling, we look around us, and behold we are held fast in the embrace of this great abyss; with walls more than half a mile high hanging directly over our heads, while the track is cut straight through the solid rock.

The canon has sharp curves, and sometimes widens out and displays steep crags that tower heavenward two or three thousand feet.

The most abrupt and isolated of these pinacles is Currecanti Needle. It has a perfect symmetry of an obelisk, composed of red sandstone, and is near 3,000 feet high.

Following the channel of the Gunnison down fifteen miles, we leave it to the right, and strike Cimarron Creek, which has a narrower channel, with walls equally as high, and nearly shut together overhead, to the bottom of which the rays of the sun never reach. Magnificence supplants detail, and the place appeals to our deepest feelings. Emerging from the canon, Cimarron Station appeared. Passing on we at once commmenced to climb the Cedar Divide, by loops, steep grades and windings, until the summit of these barren, naked and sandy-clay mountains was reached.

From here we had a fine view of the Uncompahgre Valley. Descending by looping around, we reached the plain below, which is composed of white, sandy clay, destitute of every vestige of vegetation, and nothing but utter nakedness appeared, except here and there a scattering sage. This continues ten miles to Montrose, on the Uncompahgre River, where is a little fertile spot.

Following the banks of this river ten miles more, where utter nakedness reigns, it brings us to Delta, where we strike the Gunnison River again. The lands in this great Uncompahgre Valley are rich, but will not produce the least thing without irrigation, they belong to the Ute Reservation.

Following the banks of this river 25 miles more through these rich unoccupied lands, and passing the lower canon of the Gunnison, we arrived at the Grand Junction, on the Grand River, and crossed over to the north bank. We have now reached an utter desolation. A veritable desert, continues for near 150 miles. Low, treeless, dry and neglected waste; uninhabited by man or beast. We are on a billowy desert where the winds have formed billows of sand, and not a vestige of verdure for the eye to rest upon in any direction.

We crossed the line into Utah as the sun sank beneath the horizon, away on the trackless desert. We here left the banks of the Grand River, and steered southwest to shun the Book Mountains, then bore to the northwest and crossed the Green River at Gunnison Point about 10 P. M. From here we took a northwest course, and struck the Valley of Price River, at lower Price River Crossing. From here we followed up the valley of the river till midnight, when the train stopped, and the cry was made, "behold Castle Canon, and Castle Gate, and the giant lofty cliffs and pinacles that rear their heads around you!"

We have wound and turned with the river on a gentle grade, until now we have arrived at the gateway that leads directly into the very heart of the Wasatch Mountains. In the bright starlight we viewed this stupenduous work of nature. The gateway is formed by two immense towers of red sandstone, one rising direct from the water's edge, and the other close by the side of the car track, barely leaving room between for the river and the track. They rise in open relief like obelisks, or church spires to the astonishing height of nearly 500 feet. They firmly stand upon their bases as silent sentinels of nature, placed there in the "long ago," to guide the red man through the canon to fertile fields beyond. It was down Price River Canon and past Castle Gate, that Sidney Johnson marched his army home from Utah.

When through the narrow way, we commenced to climb the steep grade of Price River Canon. The road follows one stream and then an other until we arrived at Soldier's Summit, on the very top of the range. Then like a kite in its downward flight, darting to and fro, we glide down Soldier's Canon, through the Red Narrows, Spanish Fork Canon and emerge into Utah Valley, near Utah Lake, and stop at Provo City, a favorite watering place, and one of many attractions.

The River Jordan rises in this lake, flows north into Salt Lake, separating Salt Lake Valley from Salt Lake Basin. The railway leads along the banks of the River Jordan to Salt Lake City, where I arrived at break of day Saturday, September, 29th, 1883, and by the way of our route, 2,685 miles from Utica. Since leaving the valley of the Republican River in Nebraska, for more than a thousand miles not a cultivated field has been seen, and some of the distance a parched up desert. The wealth of this region consists in the inexhaustible and untold value of its mines.

After breakfast at the Rio Grande Hotel, I went about the town, which is really a city of gardens, trees, shrubs, vines, lawns, etc.

Cereals and vegetables of all kinds are also raised. It is truly a paradise, an arcade of beauty and loveliness; where the desert blossoms like the rose. It is laid out in regular squares, with broad streets, embowered with trees, and water coursing through them all which is used for irrigating purposes; without this nothing would grow. The houses are built of wood, brick and adobe, all presenting a neat, clean and tidy appearance.

I walked into a nursery containing a great variety of fruit trees ready for transplanting, and noticing ripened fruits in an adjoining fruit garden, my footsteps led me to the door where I asked Mrs. W. L. Binder the favor of tasting the fruit of the land. She sent a secondary lady out who brought me a handful of delicious plums and a few clusters of very fine grapes. I inquired after the different varieties of fruit produced. She said, apples, pears, peaches, apricots, plums, gooseberries, currants, strawberries, raspberries, nectarines and melons of various kinds, and all of fine qualities. I also inquired a little after their domestic happiness in their mode of life. She replied we are a simple-minded people, and once trusted everybody; but have so often been betrayed that we now distrust all strangers. I told her my first season of teaching was in a settlement of friendly Mormons in the east, and I still retained that friendship, although poligamy at that time was not known in the church. She then replied, we mind our own business, let others alone, take care of all our children, and none of them are a public charge, (which many Gentiles do not do.) We support our own wives and do not ask aid from the Gentiles; yet we are constantly persecuted for our religious sentiments. To the question, how did Brigham Young find this promised land? She replied, it was revealed to Joseph Smith and he conveyed the knowledge to Brigham Young. This conversation was at Second South street, between Third and Fourth West streets.

I next walked into the beautiful flower lawns and gardens of Governor Murrey, of Utah Territory. The lawn was daily watered and the grass under my feet felt like a plush carpet. But two slight showers of rain had fallen from April to October. Flowers were abundant, pears were very fine, and grapes hung in lucious clusters, the Black Hamburg, White Muskat of Alexander, Muscatillo, and a large class of Sweetwaters. The gardener gave me a few clusters of each, and I should have called them all Sweetwaters. They made my heart glad. Mayor Jennings' residence is a very fine structure.

A few steps farther up the street I stood admiring the beautiful, unoccupied former residence of George G. T. Canon, belonging now to the church. While standing there, Mr. John Nebecker commenced conversation, which continued an hour; in which he said he was among the first to reach that place. They started in April, 1847, some in wagons, some on horseback, others on foot, and some had even hand-carts for a thousand miles' journey. An account of their toils, sufferings and privations would seem to be the exaggeration of romance. The second year after their arrival they got a little growing, and the crickets swarmed down from the mountains and commenced to devastate everything. He sat on an eminence contemplating what to do, heard a squalling, and on looking up saw a cloud of gulls that lit down and destroyed them all and the crops were saved. But sometimes they devastated everything. He said that polygamy was not at first introduced into the church, but it seemed right that all should have homes and be provided for, and no one had a right to take more wives than he could well support. I told him that women were naturally sovereign, and I could not see how it could be reconciled. He replied: True they some times are compelled to bite their lips, but being a church ordinance they endure it. He said that the very men who met in the legislature to make laws to disfranchise them, might perhaps be guilty of equal crimes, if not worse, under a different name.

Temple Square next claimed my attention. It comprises ten acres of ground, and on it are the Assembly Hall, Tabernacle and New Temple.

The Assembly Hall is built of granite, is 120 by 86 feet, and has 20 graceful minarets, each twenty feet high, and the spire has an altitude of 126 feet. The ceiling is 40 feet above the floor. The room will seat 40,000 people. The Tabernacle is a masterpiece of architectural skill. It is in oval form 250 by 150 feet on the ground. It has one great roof rounding on top, resting on 46 pillars of Red Sand Stone; and springs from side to side, and from end to end, with a single stride 80 feet above the floor, made of lattice work 10 feet thick and bolted together. It is the largest self-sustaining roof in America, except the Great Union Depot in New York. In the west end on an elevated portion stands the great organ, second in size on the continent.

On the right and left of the organ are seats for a choir of 100 persons, resting on a broad platform in front, approached by a flight of steps; at the right hand of which, and rising one above the other, are also other seats, reserved for the priests and dignitaries of the church.

The first one for the President. 2d. For the 12 Apostles. 3d. For the presidency of the High Priests and Seventies. 4th. For Bishops and Elders who administer the Sacrament, the table standing immediately in front of them, from which they administer every Sabbath afternoon.

The galleries will seat 3,750 people. The whole seating capacity is 13,452; including standing room it will accommodate 15,000 people.

There are 20 doors 9 feet wide, opening outside, and the most minute sound can be heard all over the house.

In the northwest corner of Temple Square, stands the Endowment House, where the marriages are solemnized. Strangers never enter there.

The New Temple when completed, will be one of the most substantial and beautiful edifices in the world, probably designed to stand as a monument to Brigham Young, architectural skill, perseverance and enterprise, until time shall be no more. The foundation walls are laid 16 feet below the surface, and are 16 feet in thickness, of reddish quartzite, of great hardness. The walls are built of cut stone, nine feet nine inches in thickness, of a light gray granite. The Temple is 200 feet long, 117 feet wide, and is to have three towers at each end, those on the east and west corners, to rise to an altitude of 200 feet. Each containing a stairway winding around a column four feet in diameter. The corner stone was laid April 6th, 1853.

It is estimated that it will take thirty years more to complete the work. Over $3,000.000 have already been expended. Scores of workmen add a little to it daily, and it bids fair to be the crowning glory of the west.

Crossing the street from Temple Square, I came to another walled enclosure surrounding the buildings of the late Brigham Young.

The Tithing Department, where one-tenth of all products are brought for the benefit of the church.

The Lion House and Bee Hive, two low yellow tinged, dormer windowed buildings, stand close together near the street.

The Lion House was used by President Young as an office; it is still occupied by President Taylor for the same purpose. I noticed pictures of dignitaries of the church hanging upon the walls.

In the Bee Hive President Young lived with his several wives. I walked about the yard surrounding these buildings in deep reflection.

Next to the Bee Hive is Eagle Gate, ornamented by a huge gilded eagle, resting on massive beams, that rest again on four granite posts.

On the opposite side of the road is President Taylor's residence and flower lawns. For neatness, taste, and architectual beauty, this stands first among the residences. The mercantile business of this city is immense for a city of 25,000 inhabitants.

The Zion's Co-operative Mercantile Institution, controlled by the Mormons, stands first among the business houses; it is of brick, 318 feet long by 53 feet wide, with an addition of 195 feet long by 25 feet wide. The Waker Brothers have a large mercantile business, and the sales of the two aggregate over $5,000,000 yearly.

One of Zions clerk's took me through their departments, and from the third story window I had a fine view of Fort Douglass. The market is supplied with everything that heart could wish.

At 4.45 p. m., I took the cars for Great Salt Lake, which is one of the great wonders of creation. The mystery brooding around it, the learned can not dispel; no matter how able their theories may be.

This lake has various rivers of fresh water constantly pouring into it but none running from it. The water is so salt that fish can not live in it, being about one-fourth per cent; and so dense that its surface is seldom ruffled by the wind. Spread out like a mighty mirror, it lies inert, simmering in the sunlight all the day. On the mountains surrounding it, are three distinct water washes, which show that the lake has receded from its original bounds, or the mountains have been raised up by volcanic action. Turning our thoughts again to the cars we passed through sage bush twenty miles to the foot of the Wasatch mountains where we struck the lake. The dressing rooms were opened, the bathing suits adjusted, and fourteen gentlemen and six ladies appeared on the platform ready for the water. As the gentlemen led the young ladies down a flight of stairs, their elastic steps, well rounded forms, and delicate limbs, indicated that they were as fleet as the wild Gazelle; and I expected to see them shoot away like some fairy nymph of the deep. But O! with all their model forms and symetrical beauty, they were not experts in swimming. They universally swam on their backs, lying straight as a board on the water; making no motions with their feet, merely paddling with their hands over their heads. Returned at 8 P. M.

Brigham Young did not encourage prospecting for minerals; but since the advent of the railroads the attention of the people has turned in that direction. Rich deposits of gold, silver, lead, iron, copper, coal, zinc, cinnabar, antimony, brimstone, gypsum, soda and some others, have been developed, and yield rich returns. Salt can be shoveled up about Salt Lake, and as the lake is 90 miles long and 40 miles wide, and one-fourth of its bulk actual salt, the nation is provided with this article for untold ages. Utah will soon be numbered among the richest mining division of the Union.

Sunday September 30, at 2 P. M., I was seated by Mr. John Nebecker, in the Mormon Tabernacle, directly in front of the choir, and dignitaries of the church. President Taylor entering the door, the choir accompanied by the organ, rendered the hymn, "Earth with its Ten Thousand Flowers."

Prayer by Herbert Grant, followed by music again, "How Dark and Dreary was the Night."

The seven Bishops then broke the bread, instead of cutting it. Thanks was then rendered; and while the bread was being passed through the multitude, a son of the late Brigham Young arose and said, in some respects I am pleased to address you, I, in connection with others have received a revelation that the second coming of Christ is at hand.

I am not taught that those out of the church of the Latter Day Saints are destined to destruction, but that all shall receive according to their works. We believe that we lived before we were born; and shall live on after death; and live here again. We have no knowledge of what was before birth, but shall know after death.

This is a probationary state to know good from evil, and, to prepare for an everlasting existence. A state of trial to prove ourselves, and listen to the spirit of revelation. People call that spirit conscience. Joseph Smith, when a boy but 14 years of ag, directed by inspiration to the book of Mormon. And his prophecies, that we should multiply and become a mighty people, and build up Zion in the west, it is a prophecy that I have lived to see fulfilled.

On the 24th day of July, 1847, 143 men came down yonder canon on to a desert plain 1,000 miles from any civilized abode, and in 30 years they numbered 143,000. In 30 years more, at the same ratio we shall number 143,000,000. This people will honor the laws that be, but in time they will govern the nation. A moment's pause and a blessing was asked on the water, the bishops then served it.

In 1843, Joseph Smith and John Fessidan prophesied that a war would be waged in our midst, and this was familiar with us until it took place. And still destruction awaits this nation unless they repent. Joseph Smith sacrificed his life to save the people. We send out our elders, and people deride us for sending out ignorant men. If we could save the money we are forced to spend in the law, we could educate all the children in the country. I have known nothing but persecution on account of plural marriage. But who has violated the law of 1882 ? I am disfranchised. I am no man. I have been voted out of existence. What can I do now with my three wives and four sons?

Joseph Nicholson then arose and preached a regular discourse, being so near allied to what we hear in other churches, I took few notes; still I noticed that he said, the latter day saints claim that the prophecies of the scriptures are fulfilled in these latter days. We also claim to preach the same gospel that was preached by the Apostles; yet we are set aside without investigation, persecuted and disfranchised unheard. They closed by singing, which was quite sublime.

From whence did this sect arise that has turned the world upside down ? Joseph Smith, born in Vermont, removed to central New York, and at the age of 15, commenced to see mysterious things in vision. At the age of 22 he declared he had a revelation from on high, making known to him the hiding place of a metal book, written with Egyptian characters, which Smith pretended to translate—the mysterious "Book of Mormon"—and declared it to be a new gospel. I have read some in the book. It is written in the style of the Old Testament of our Bible. His followers did not discard our Bible, but always preached from it, and claimed to adhere closely to its teachings; yet still held that the "Book of Mormon" was an accompaniment. It has been said by some that the "Book" was written by a man named Spaulding, yet I think it was never proven.

Smith called his followers to Jackson County, the extreme western portion of Missouri, and told them all the western country was designed for their inheritance. In 1833 he had 1,200 followers. This sudden influx of polygamists excited jealousy in the minds of the Missourians, and they rose in a body, and without resistance drove them all out of the State. They migrated east, crossed the Mississippi a little above the mouth of the Des Moines River into

Illinois, where on a bluff, they formed the beautiful city of Nauvoo in 1840, erecting there a magnificent temple. Large numbers flocked to their city; including men of wealth and influence, until they numbered 10,000. The Illinoisians became suspicious of their increasing power, brought accusations against the Mormons and their leaders, arrested Joseph Smith and his brother, and incarcerated them at Carthage. The popular fury was so great that a mob broke into the jail, and murdered them both on July 7th, 1844. Joseph Smith's cloak, at his death, fell upon Brigham Young. The odium against them was so great, and persecution so virulent, that they eventually sold their possessions in Illinois and deserted their city.

Brigham Young at once stepped to the front, seized the helm, and rescued the church from utter dissolution. He called the chief dignitaries together, laid his plans before them to migrate to Mexico Territory, and build up Zion in the Valley of Great Salt Lake, entirely isolated, 1,000 miles from any civilization. It is a miracle of miracles, how they ever accomplished this journey over the Rocky Mountains, and across the plains.

Brigham Young, late president and prophet of the Mormon "Church of the Latter Day Saints," was born in Vermont, June 1st, 1801. Reared a Methodist, occupation a carpenter. Married in 1824, and in 1830 first saw "The Book of Mormon." In 1832 he was baptized by Joseph Smith and became a member of the church, the good of which was always the first and foremost in all his undertakings. He possessed decision of character, yet at the same time the more tender and moral virtues, a great financier, a promoter of "internal improvements," a natural architect, a man of the soundest judgment, his plans when carried out always accomplishing the end for which they were laid. He was far seeing, and could look to the end before the beginning was commenced. He was venturous, and plunged into the most obscure plans and always came out in daylight on the other side.

On July 24th, 1847, he arrived at Great Salt Lake Valley, the sage covered plain, where few had ever trod, and on July 21st, Great Salt Lake City was laid out. In 1848 the Republic of Mexico ceded the territory to the United States.

In 1850 President Fillmore appointed Brigham Young governor of Utah Territory. The Mormons afterwards were not willing to recognize any other authority, and set at defiance the jurisdiction of the United States over them.

In the fall of 1857 President Buchanan dispatched 2,500 men to enforce acknowledgment. While in winter quarters, embassadors were sent to the Mormons with proposals of pardon in case of their acknowledging the authority of the government. They accepted the terms.

In 1862 Joseph Morris rose up and claimed to be the true Prophet of God instead of Brigham Young. He had 390 followers. The Mormon Legions under Robert T. Burton attacked them in their defenceless state, shot down their leader, Joseph Morris, and twenty or thirty more. The Morrisites were then all taken to Salt Lake City as slaves.

In March, 1863, Hon. S. S. Harding arrived as Governor, and pardoned them all.

Brigham Young has taken a conspicuous part in every public improvement, assisting in forming stage lines and express companies, and when the Union Pacific Railroad was being built, he graded 150 miles of track, erected several hundred miles of the Western Union Telegraph, and was first and foremost in every laudable pursuit. He built the Brigham Young Academy at Provo, and amply endowed it some years before his death. And later in life he deeded a farm near Logan City, of 9,643 acres, under a good state of cultivation, to trustees in trust, to endow a college located at that city, to be called "Brigham Young College."

August 29th., 1877, at the age of 76, he died, deeply regretted by his followers, and much admired by the world at large. His name will ever stand upon the pages of history, as one of the most remarkable men of the 19th century.

I sought his resting-place; and passing through the Eagle Gate near the Bee Hive, walked up a narrow street, turned to the right, and entered a walled enclosure, which is divided into four parts; three of which lay waste. It is a private burying-ground.

The southeast quarter is covered with a grass lawn, destitute of shrubs or flowers, but tastefully divided up by concrete walks. Close in the south-east corner of this lawn is a hidden vault of mason work, covered with a large flag-stone, on which stands an ornamental iron picketed railing. Beneath this stone, silent and alone, without a word to tell of his eventful life, in peace rests the ashes of the late priest and prophet, Brigham Young. I bowed over the railing in deep and solemn thought. The great has fallen. An active, busy life has closed. I have tried to tell his virtues. Others have labored harder to inflate his vices. Here, now, side by side, both virtues and vices, with his ashes rest. And the great Ruler above, only, has the right to judge between.

Near the close of the day I took the street car to the medical warm springs. The water has a temperature of 102 degrees F., and is used much in plunge baths. The hot springs are about three miles farther on, having a temperature of 180 F., and are not a watering place, neither do street cars approach any nearer. Supposing this to be the objective point when taking the cars, I proposed to walk the remaining portion. The boys would not go. I arrived about sunset. The springs flow out directly from the foot of the mountain, 1,200 feet above; forming a stream six inches deep and several feet wide. There is a green, slimy substance surrounding the spring, and the water was so hot I could not hold my hand in it.

Returning, when I entered the city it was dark, and the thick growth of trees on both sides the streets, added much to the opaqueness of the scene. Weary and thirsty, I stopped at a house for drink. The floor was carpeted, a piece of music stood there, and everything was neat and in order, and bespoke the greatest degree of domestic happiness. Her husband was one of the bishops. There are 21 wards in the city, and a bishop in each one. I told her I had nothing against their doctrine and religion except polygamy, and that I could not recognize. She said she was one of two wives, and it was not always pleasant, but it was an ordinance of the church, and they submitted to it. One word more and I leave the subject. Light dispels darkness, and this institution will soon vanish away. I found my way to the Rio Grande Hotel—Joseph Smith proprietor—and retired for the night.

Monday, October 1st, 1883.—At 7 A. M. I took my way through a cultivated, broad expansive plain, 36 miles north to Ogden. This is the junction of the Union and Central Pacific railroads, 1,032 miles from Omaha, and from San Francisco, 882. The Utah Central, and the Utah Northern railroads also have a junction here, and things of every nature change cars. A full hour here gives passengers ample time to eat a good square meal for $1.00. The citizens are Mormons, have a tabernacle, and all public improvements are supervised by them. Population, 6,500. Irrigation has made it one great garden of fruit and flowers.

All on board, we started west, having Great Salt Lake on the left, and the Wasatch Mountains on the right, rising thousands of feet above us. Some hundreds of feet up on the side of the mountains, plainly visible from the cars, is seen the old water wash of the lake, stretching along in one unbroken line for many miles, which shows that this lake was once a mighty sea, in the untold millions of ages past, and covered all the Great American Desert, Salt Lake Valley, and all of Great Salt Lake Basin. This is no creation of the imagination. The well worn rocks, pebbles, and lines of marine shells, demonstrate this fact beyond question. Below the first line are two more, which show that the lake had three altitudes before reaching its present level. Advancing fifteen miles farther we arrived at the Mormon town of Willard, containing 700 inhabitants. On the mountain near by is the crater of an extinct volcano. All is barren, and lava lies around it.

Brigham is the next Mormon town, embowered in fruit trees. They have a tabernacle, but no saloons. Population, 1,800

Call's Fork is noted for its many springs flowing from the base of the mountain, some cold, others very hot; also for alkali beds.

The road now crosses Bear River, on a trestle bridge, 1,200 feet long, over water 18 feet deep, and brings us to Corinne, 24 miles from Ogden. Thus far we have followed close by the side of the Utah Northern, which now turns directly north and leaves us. The water of the Malad River is brought 11 miles to the city, irrigating thousands of acres, and propelling a mill that produces four tons of flour daily.

Westward we strike the white, barren alkali beds near the lake, and the excavated channel beside the road is filled with a reddish looking water. One sip of it satisfies a man for a lifetime. After following these loathsome deposits along the lake 20 miles, we cross Blue Creek, on a trestle bridge, 300 feet long and 30 feet high.

Then we begin to climb Promontory Mountain, by winding and

turning, and through deep rock cuts, up, up we go, until we reach the former terminus of the two roads, 1,084 miles from Omaha, and 830 miles from San Francisco. Here, on the 10th day of May, 1869, were gathered people from the four quarters of the globe, to witness the connection of this iron line across the continent. The last tie was made of California laurel, plated with silver. The last rails were laid by parties from both companies. There was then provided a gold spike from California, a silver one from Nevada, and one of gold, silver and iron from Arizona. A hammer of silver was also in readiness, and at 12 m. the blows were struck that connected the link, and the telegraph wires throughout the Union quivered with the glad intelligence, while cheer after cheer, rent the air. From here we had a down grade eight miles, and struck the lake again, and travel on the shore 16 miles to Monument, where alkaline and saline odors are offensive to invalids.

Monument Point is a slim, tapering promontory stretching far out into the lake, covered with grass, the last we shall see for many a mile, as we are now about to enter the Great American Desert. A run of 14 miles more carried us around the shore of the western arm of the lake, and we saw it no more.

Kelton stands on the edge of the desert. It has large water tanks supplied from springs some miles north. Here the railroad company fill their water cars daily, to supply the stations on the desert. We launched out from Kelton as into an open sea, having mountains all the time in sight on the right, and the desert on our left appearing as though the lake had lately covered it, and receded far back many miles out of sight, leaving a white salt beach, as smooth as a plained floor.

The alkali spreads over the broad, smooth surface of apparent beds of rivers all perfectly dry, and as white as the driven snow. The eye then wandered on in search of some green thing, or something to show that life or vegetation ever existed there. All is desolate in the extreme, one broad, expansive waste of apparent salt, spread out as smooth as a canvas, glistening in the sun, until at last the vision meets the horizon. This desert was evidently once the bed of Great Salt Lake, and it slightly slopes that way. The same water wash that was seen at Ogden has continued, and can be distinctly traced on the same level all the way.

For the next 60 miles which carries us to the Nevada line, the country is somewhat mountainous and broken, yet it can be said to be but little or nothing less than one continuous barren, desolate waste, not capable of supporting human life. At the Nevada line is a castle rock, rising directly from the plain, in a symetrical form like a church spire, to an altitude of several hundred feet.

Pilot's Peak, that has been seen for the last 50 miles, is now near at hand on the left, 2,500 feet above the plain.

Nevada has mines of silver and coal, but raising of stock is the chief occupation of the inhabitants. Twenty-five miles more brought us to Cedar Pass, which divides the desert from Humboldt Valley.

The dreary waste, with its marine shells and fossilized fragments of past ages, is exchanged for vegetation and fountains of water. From the summit of Cedar Pass, we had a down grade 311 miles, following the valley of the Humboldt River to Humboldt Sink, from whence the waters never flow. Crossing and re-crossing the river half a dozen times on our journey. Humboldt Wells are 2,940 miles from Utica, and 664 miles from San Francisco, where the emigrants stopped to rest and recruit after their long and toilsome journey across the parching desert. There are about 20 of these wells gently flowing. They have been sounded to a depth of 20,000 feet, yet no bottom has been reached. They are supposed to be the craters of extinct volcanoes, as masses of lava, and broken fragments of rocks are hurled in chaotic confusion all over the surrounding country. Night had gathered around us, but still we moved on down the grade, and soon struck the valley of the Humboldt river. This valley is extremely rich, but the seasons are too short for cultivation.

Elco is noted for its shipment of cattle, which numbers more than any other station on the road. The annual shipments from the valley are 500 car loads. Near Elco are the celebrated medical springs, some are so hot as to be used for natural cauldrons to cook food. In Hot Springs Valley, eight miles from our road, are an hundred hot springs, some of which spout water 30 feet in the air. There are many other hot springs in Nevada, but we pass them by and look for the cause that produces the heat. The ignorant suppose they are places of escape for steam from water heated by the internal fires forever burning below. Learned philosophers argue that mineral in solution in water, causes all the disturbance. Yet I have found some that apparently hold no mineral in solution, which explodes their reasoning, while a third class religiously think it proceeds from a place prepared for the wicked. One knows about as much as the other. We followed the valley of the Humboldt river all night, in its windings and turnings, passing some sublime scenery, arriving at the town of Humboldt for breakfast. Looking forward, nothing could be seen but barenness, and desolation, and we learned we were on the edge of the Great Nevada Desert, having passed 300 miles of producing country since leaving the Great American Desert. Passing on again we soon came opposite Humboldt Lake, 35 miles long and 10 miles wide, lying in the Great Nevada Basin, and has no outlet. It is still an unsolved problem what becomes of its waters, as the Humboldt river, 350 miles long, with all its tributaries from the mountains, is constantly pouring its waters in, and the Carson river on the south discharging a large volume of water also into its bosom, yet it never rises beyond its bounds. There are many lakes of the same character in the Great Basin, their waters being slightly brackish and all having no outlets.

Leaving Humboldt and Carson lakes behind, we move directly out on to the desert which is composed of brown hills, barren sandy plains, lakes without outlets, large deposits of by gone ages, mixed with clay, which can not vegetate. Fossil remains bearing evidence of past submersion, one dreary expansive waste, destitute of wood and water. At White Plains, the surface is crusted over with alkali, sloping off towards the lakes, and the sun shines on it with burning rays. Here is where the early traveler so often chased the phantom seen in the distance, green fields and rivers of water. This optical delusion is called mirage, and has led many a traveler astray to perish on the burning sands.

This Great Desert Basin extends from Oregon on the north, crossing Nevada and Arizona into Mexico. It bears the same characteristics all the way, viz.; lava beds, alkali flats, hot springs, barren wastes, cheerless and desolate.

We stopped at Reno on the west side of the Desert for dinner, which cost a dollar, a cup of coffee alone twenty-five cents. Reno is a business place at the junction of Virginia and Truckee railroad with the Central Pacific, and has a population of 1,500.

We are now at the base of the Sierra Nevada mountains, and have a heavy up grade, 48 miles to the summit.

Our course leads along up the canon of the Truckee River which has its source in Lake Tahoe, where immense quantities of logs are cut, and floated through the lake, and down the stream, to mills along its course.

The Truckee canon is deep and narrow, having no valley, adown which the waters of the river rush and foam, with terrific force. Unnumbered saw-mills are located along its banks, the mountains on both sides are well timbered, and sloping back with numerous gorges and ravines, affording ample facility for flumes, through which lumber is floated down from the mills far back on the mountains above. These flumes are common in all the lumber sections, throughout the mountain regions. Some of them are more than 20 miles in length. The water is taken in from some small stream near the summit, the lumber placed in the troughs and gently borne down to the stations below. All logs within short distances of the river are tumbled down its banks, or run down on slides, and plunged into the river, the great thoroughfare for logs along its banks, as well as all those from Lake Tahoe.

Continuing up this water course 26 miles we crossed the State Line into California, and ten miles farther brought us to Truckee City. Along through all this distance is one continuous scene of lumbering. Lumber, ties, logs and wood, in places seem almost to choke up the way. This city has 2,000 inhabitants all of whom are connected with the lumber trade. It is twelve miles north of Lake Tahoe, that great summer resort, and two miles from Donner Lake, where Mr. Donner and his wife perished from starvation in the winter of 1846.

We will now take leave of Truckee City and start for the summit of the Sierras, 14 miles distant, having two strong locomotives attached to draw us up the steep grades.

Pine forests, jagged peaks, deep gorges, rocky cliffs, and nature's wildest scenery greets us on every hand.

We wound around Donner Lake Valley and entered the snow sheds, which with the numerous long tunnels forms an unbroken line of 45 miles. As we toiled along up, by looking through the peek-holes in the sheds, we saw vistas of Donner Lake lying hundreds of feet below, with its mirrored surface covered with ice closely nestling beneath the surrounding pine clad peaks, and sadly thought of Donner's fate, perishing under 20 feet snow.

Up, up, higher and more high we toiled until arriving at the summit where the side track is also covered by the snow sheds.

This is the highest point of the Central Pacific Railroad, altitude 7,017 feet. Distance from Utica by our route 3,359 miles. Distance from San Francisco 245 miles.

The snow sheds are built of strong timber with one roof so that avalanches will slide directly over them.

Soda Springs on the summit is said to be equal to any manufactured soda water.

Now, descending a rapid grade, winding, turning and looping around spurs of the mountains, we at length reached Blue Canon where a number of saw mills are located, from which large quantities of lumber are shipped.

The scenery has been weird, ever changing and beautiful over the mountains, but the culminating point is yet to come.

Passing Shady Run we saw on our left one of the grandest scenes in the Sierra Nevada Mountains. The Great American Canon two miles long, with smooth perpendicular granite walls rising 2,000 feet directly out of the water. The walls are compressed so near together that the water washes each side, and no person has ever yet been able to pass through the gorge, even on foot.

While steadfastly gazing, the train bears to the right, and is lost to sight. We are now approaching the Blue Lode placier mining district, which extends through Nevada and Sierra counties, and is from 100 to 500 feet below the surface, and from one to five miles wide. It is supposed to be the bed of some ancient river, which is demonstrated by finding petrified trees lying at the bottom, some of them six feet through and of the same variety as now grow on the surface. A field for thought, yet none can tell the ages past.

Hydraulic mining is carried on by bringing streams down the mountains in flumes and ditches for many miles, then attaching a hose to the flume with an iron nozzle through which the water rushes, tearing down the banks, gravel and stone, wash down through a tail race into a long flume where the riffles for collecting gold are placed. The mountain sides are lined with these water courses, and an army of men are at work, who live in little cozy cabins, but no children are seen about their doors. Going down the mountain rapidly amid mining claims, by the side of long ditches through the deep gravel cuts, until all at once the north fork of the American River broke on our sight, dashing and foaming in a narrow gorge 1,500 feet below us. As we rounded the point of a mountain on a narrow rim cut along its side and looked down upon the peaks below, with a deep gorge winding its way between,.we were at once struck with wonder and astonishment at the grandeur and sublimity of the scene, while every moment brought some new object to our vision. The canon breaks on our sight again, and this time almost directly under us, 2,500 feet below. Slowly we moved along, looking down upon the stream that appeared like a rivulet in the chasm below.

' This is Cape Horn, one of the grandest scenes on the globe. Timid ladies took one look and nerveless fell back to their seats again. Their vision could not linger on this awe inspiring grandeur, which tongue can not tell, or pen portray.

In the distance far below we saw a dark strip like a plank spanning the stream. We learned it was the turnpike bridge leading to Iowa Hill. Turning around and looking up the mountain from whence we came, we saw merely a rim on its steep side where the Indian could not make a foot trail; but our brave men were fastened by ropes until they could get a footing. We have now passed around that dizzy height in safety, and viewed from 3,000 feet below, the cars appear to be rolling through the clouds. Below us still we see the road bed running in opposite directions, but at length reaching it, where we crossed Rice's Ravine, on a trestle bridge, 113 feet high and 878 long, under which the Colfax and Nevada road passes. This is a three-foot narrow gauge, and is 22½ miles long. The scenery along its line is said to be passingly sublime.

Leaving Colfax, we leave the towering, rugged peaks behind, and follow down the foot hills, 10 miles to Clipper Gap, then onward still, passing through many an old washed placer mine, where not long ago could be seen thousands of men digging and washing from early dawn until darkness shrouded the west, seeking for the "root of all evil." It is a thing of the past, all dug over, now lies desolate.

Along the foot hill of the range, gardens, orchards and vineyards abound, and all betoken happiness and quiet.

A few miles more brought us to Roseville Junction, of the Oregon division. We have now struck the great Sacramento Valley where grain, orchards, and vineyards abound, and return a hundred fold. Passed one vineyard of 110 acres in which the grapes were laid on boards to dry for raisins. Near by was an orchard of 400 acres, all set with Bartlett pears. Sacramento is situated on the east bank of the Sacramento River near its confluence with the American. It is a thriving and flourishing city. Population, 23,000. It contains the State Capitol and county buildings.

The Johnson and Brandy-Wine Company work 400 tons of grapes annually. The beet sugar factory has a capacity of 100 tons daily, employing 500 hands. The woolen mills work 1,000 pounds daily. All the cars used on the road are built here, and the company has a hospital erected where the sick and unfortunate are cared for. The river bed has been filled up from 12 to 18 feet by debris washed down from the mines above, which render levees necessary.

c

Now, right here, let me stop on my journey, and bestow my sympathy on General Sutter, the pioneer of California, who first unearthed the shining dust, that set the world ablaze.

We will go up the Sacramento River 25 miles to the confluence of the Feather River, then up that stream 20 miles to the Hock Farm, the home of the venerable pioneer of California, General Sutter. The old farmhouse and iron fort remain. Enormous fig-trees, orchards and vineyards are still flourishing, planted by the General more than 50 years ago. General Sutter received his grant from the Russian Government, which conveyed to him the site of Sacramento City, and land for 30 or 40 miles around it; of which the Hock Farm is a part. Swindlers deprived him of his property, and he died penniless, a pensioner on the State.

The first gold was discovered January 19th, 1848, by J. W. Marshall, in General Sutter's mill-race.

A description of the products, wealth and enterprise from Sacramento to San Francisco would fill a volume. Suffice it to say, this, in connection with many other parts of California, is the garden spot of the earth. I will only mention a few of its products, and the large scale on which they are raised.

On the west side of the Sacramento River and extending north a hundred miles, is one continuous line of wheat fields. Across the river on the east side Mr. Briggs has a small farm of wheat land containing 30,000 acres, producing from 30 to 50 bushels to the acre.

Now, coming directly to the line of our road, we will notice the fruit along its course. Alameda County lying between San Francisco Bay and San Joaquin River, has a deep, rich, alluvial soil, which is adapted to the growth of all kinds of fruit, and vegetables, The size, weight and quality are truly marvelous, and an account of it, to us, seems almost fabulous. One man, a Mr. Meek, has a 2,200 acre farm here. On 300 of which are 250,000 currant bushes, 1,200 almond trees, 4,200 cherry trees, 8,000 prune and plum trees, 1,500 pear trees, 2,500 apple trees, 1,800 peach trees, 2,000 apricot trees and 60 acres in blackberries, besides large orange groves.

Another man raised in 1877, 200 tons of pumpkins, 300 tons of beets and 200 tons of carrots.

Currants grow as big as filberts and cherries measure 3 inches in circumference. All the tree fruits are astonishingly large, and the mammoth size and weight of vegetables we scarcely dare tell. Carrots grow three feet long and weigh 35 pounds, cabbage weigh 75 pounds, onions 5 pounds, watermelons 85 pounds, pears $3\frac{1}{2}$ pounds, strawberries two ounces and beets 200 pounds. These beat all other beets on earth.

From Sacramento our course led directly south to Stockton, on the San Joaquin River at the head of navigation. The town has a great trade in grain, and a population of 13,000. The city is supplied with water from an artesian well, 1,002 feet deep, which discharges 360,000 gallons of water daily. The water rises 10 feet above the surface. We still continued south to Lathrop, where we struck the Visalia division, then turned in a westerly course to Oakland. The city of Oakland is the second in size on the Pacific coast, having a population of 35,000, and has arisen as by magic in the last few years. It derives its name from the live oaks in its vicinity. Orchards, parks and vineyards are on every hand, and it nestles in perpetual verdure, and is the residence of the wealthy of San Francisco.

The State Asylum for the deaf, blind and dumb is a fine three story, stone building, located here, surrounded by a park with beds of flowers and bowers of grapes, around and among which the inmates were walking, and apparently enjoying life cheerily.

Manufactures have received much attention, $4,350,000 are invested in that enterprise.

Moving slowly through the town, the train ran on to a long pier, extending half way across San Francisco Bay, and there we were transferred to the ferry-boat, from the upper deck of which two mighty cities could be seen. Oakland behind us, San Francisco before us, containing 240,000 inhabitants from every land and clime on the face of the globe. When gold was first discovered in 1848, there were not 500 white people in as many hundred miles, and ships seldom touched its shores. It now holds commerce with all the world. Nearly all the railroads have been built in the same time, and here they all end.

From the creation of the world, no nation ever before made such progress. We go with electricity, and time and space are annihilated. Thirty years more, who can tell?

Collecting my thoughts, I looked to the right and saw Goat Island a mass of naked rock, 340 feet high, containing 350 acres. Then turning around I notice we were at the city of San Francisco. I took an omnibus, went up into the city and took rooms at the Prescott House. The word up when applied to many of the streets of this city is very appropriate. The grades of some of the street-walks are so rapid that they are ascended all the way by flights of wooden steps. The first object that attracted my attention in the city, was some beautiful little palace street cars, passing up and down steep grades without horse or steam or any visible propelling power. Under the paving is an endless cable in motion, and over that is a cleft in the road-bed, two inches wide, and extending the entire length of the line. A grappling iron extends down through the car and also through the cleft below, where it grasps the cable, and its gentle motion moves the car forward.

Wednesday, October 3d, I went out to view the city. It is very substantially built. Mostly of iron, brick and stone.

The first house was built in 1835, then called Yuba Buna. Changed to San Francisco, in 1847. There are churches of all kinds, including several " Joss Houses," and it is also well supplied with schools and 65 periodicals are published there.

The market is filled with the choicest fruits in the world, and abundance of everything else. There are three Chinese theaters,

where their vain tricks are performed which are as dead to us as
their language.

The public buildings are numerous, large and beautiful; a
description of which would fill a volume. I will describe but one.
The Palace Hotel—which I visited many times—the largest in the
world, covers an entire square. Market, New Montgomery
Jessie and Annie streets surround it. It is 344 feet by 265, and
seven stories high, (115 feet.) The foundations are 12 feet thick.
The walls outside and in, are banded together with iron, and on the
upper story the bands are but two feet apart. The roof is tin and
glass. and cornice zinc and iron. It has three courts, one 144 by
84 feet. The water comes from four artesian wells, with a capacity
of 28,000 gallons per hour. The base reservoir contains 630,000
gallons, and one on the roof 128,000. It is supplied with five
elevators and all the modern improvements.

From here I went to China Town, which comprises three streets
occupied exclusively by Heathen Chinese shop-keepers. The buildings are the same as in other parts of the city—all else, how
different! It seemed like stepping at once to the opposite side of
the globe. They all dress in their native Chinese style, with blue
pants, a loose frock coming to the hips, sandals on their feet, with
a thick springy sole that gives elasticity to their steps and causes
them to out walk the other citizens. A round cap, tassle and
cue finishes up their rig. Chinamen live on a little. If I were
forced to live as they do, I should live on less. I noticed in their
market, strings of dried meat, and fish from the larger down to
the least minnows, as dry as a husk. Also dried fowls and smoked
meats of different kinds, and some unmentionable things. The
vegetables were many of them foreign to me. The whole looked
loathsome. I retired at the Prescott House for the night.

Thursday, October 4th, the street cars carried me to the flower
gardens of Frank Pixley, editor of the *Argonaut*, in the western
addition, occupying one entire square. Roses and thousands of
other flowers are growing, among which I noticed the Flora Pango,
producing the largest flower I ever saw, and of a pure white, bell-
shaped, 10 inches in length, and six inches broad at the mouth—
very odorous. Fuchsias grow to be a shrub 10 or 12 feet high,
and pinks abound all the year.

Leaving this lovely spot I climbed a high elevation and veiwed
the surroundings, the bay and the Golden Gate. Passing on to
Gerry street, I took another cable five miles, then stage 3½ miles
to the Cliff House, standing on a bluff 200 feet high, where the
briny waves of the Pacific Ocean lash the rock-bound shore, dashing spray into the air.

The Cliff House is a large, commodious and fashionable resort.
On entering the same I heard a noise from the backside which
sounded as though all the donkeys in San Francisco were holding
carnival with a herd of swine, and the dogs of Lapland and Siberia
were hurrying them on into the Pacific Ocean. Passing to the

veranda facing the briny deep, I saw before me three small rocky islands, rising directly from the water, and but 500 yards away. They are called the Seal Islands, and there was the seal revelry. Their number was legion, for they could not be counted. There seemed to be much rivalry among them to see which could climb the highest. One called General Grant, weighing about 3,000 pounds lay on top of the rocks 200 feet above Yeo-Hoeing, but none of the rest, in their efforts, could ascend to him. They were all over the rocks in every direction. Some going up, others plunging off, growling, barking and quarrelling. Leaving this scene of life and animation, I walked down the cliff to the sandy beach beyond, where, in stricken awe, I viewed Old Pacific's surges roll, and felt a Maker's power, then bowed and owned my nothingness

The Golden Gate is a channel of water a mile wide that connects San Francisco Bay with the ocean. Upon the bluffs 100 feet above the water are stratas of shell and bone two feet thick. Drift sand extends back from the lower beach some miles, and is carried into ridges by the wind like drifts of snow, having not a vestige of vegetation.

Returning to the city I changed my lodgings to the International Hotel, which is advertised to be fire and earthquake proof.

Friday, October 5th, I bought a return ticket, unlimited, paid $122.10. Spent the day in the city collecting information respecting excursions, and put up at the International Hotel.

Saturday, October 6th, I started for Mountain View Cemetery and Piedmont White Sulphur Springs. Crossing the ferry to Oakland, I first viewed a beautiful flower garden, before which in the street stands the eucalyptus, or blue gum trees, which are natives of Australia, where they attain a height of 300 feet, and are from 12 to 15 feet in diameter. They flourish without irrigation, with astonishing rapidity, on all kinds of California soil. Millions of them are being set for their shade, timber and medical qualities, which are very great in preventing malarial diseases. Those spoken of have been planted 14 years, are 80 feet high, and 82 inches around the base. It is an evergreen tree, with leaves 10 inches long.

\ Now starting on again, a street car took me five miles to Mountain View, where following up a drive one-fourth of a mile to the place of interment, on both sides of which, and continuing the entire length, are rose bushes and geraniums thickly set and laden with flowers. Rising from among these, and at certain intervals throughout the line, the tall pampa grass waves its chaste head over the emblems of purity that hang clustered below. A fountain with jets of water rising high in the air, is located at the upper end of the drive. The basin swarming with gold fish, and surrounded by fuchsias, bowing their modest heads, as if to drink in the water below. For beauty of walks and drives, it rivals Greenwood. Spreading palms are set about the grounds, and on the hill sides are thick groves of eucalyptus trees. Colton's monument, the most noted, is in the form of a cottage, built of marble, 14 by 18 feet, pillars in front, with capitals. The only inscription "Our Beloved Colton."

From these grounds I walked towards the Piedmont White Sulphur Springs. On my way thither I passed an orchard bowed down with choicest fruit. The kind lady of the house, with a smile, granted me the freedom of the grounds, and all the products I desired. Such rich and luscious fruit I had not tasted since my childhood days.

Reaching the Spring House, fifteen cents was demanded, entrance fee, the ticket good also for that amount in the dining room. The springs were mere nothing. The bill of fare in the dining room ran from a dollar down, but did not reach the ticket. I paid the balance, smiling at the shrewdness of the arrangement, as a second call would scarcely be made. A grove of a hundred acres of eucalyptus trees standing back on the mountain was all the redeeming qualities I could see. I returned to the National Hotel San Francisco.

Sunday, October 7th.—Weary of city confusion, I thought to spend a portion of the day in reflection among the big red woods in the wilderness, and on the ocean beach at Santa Cruz. Through Alameda the eucalyptus trees are planted by the side of the track. The company have near a million of them in nursery stock, and intend to set them the entire length of their lines.

Passing the noted Alameda baths, the road led out upon the salt marsh, where were seen stacks of salt, resembling the white tents of a soldiers' camp. No sheds being necessary to cover it, as no rain falls from April to November. Wild fowls on these marshes are legion.

At Alvarado are the beet sugar mills, consuming 25 tons of coal a day, manufacturing immense quantities of sugar. From here to San Jose, 25 miles, is a level country, the Santa Clara Valley, the garden of California, a second Eden.

Sacks filled with potatoes and onions, setting upright, stretched in long rows across the fields, and the varieties of fruit are various. Such as strawberries, tomatoes, almonds, filberts, pecans, walnuts, peppers, persimmons, prunes, pomegranates, oranges, lemons, figs, apricots, and above all grapes.

San Jose city has a population of 18,000, being the fourth in the State. It was settled by Spanish missionaries in 1777. The Alameda grove was planted in 1799—a pretty grove and a handsome city. We had an up-grade to Los Gatos, the natural home of the grape. From here we began our ascent of the Santa Cruz Mountains, following Los Gatos Creek and passing through eight tunnels and under the summit of the mountain, making our egress on the other side in the red wood forest, where large quantities of lumber are floated down in flumes from mills far back in the mountains. The scenery through this rugged pass is awfully sublime, assuming all manner of shapes and forms that the imagination can conceive. Descending, we followed Bean Creek and the Zayante Creek through the red wood forest to Falton, where they join the San Lorenzo River that passes through the Big Tree Grove, then on to Santa Cruz—the City of the Holy Cross. Arriving here the ocean forbid our farther progress.

I walked upon the beach where God had marked the sea its bounds, and looked away upon the deep to see its troubled waters roll. Turning around and viewing the town, I saw it scattered over hill and dale, completely embowered in fruit trees, vines and flowers. Surrounded on three sides by mountains and forest, with the broad ocean in front. I saw on the hill-side a low cottage just peeping out above the many shrubs, vines and flowers, that surrounded it. Finding my way there, a lady presented me a fine bouqet. I noticed among the rest a cactus two feet in circumference, and ten feet high, laden with fruit said to be very good, but should not be eaten in the dark. I walked through orchards and gardens where the branches bowed down with fruit, and was made welcome to all I desired. Baldwins and greenings I noticed were cultivated and rather put the blush on ours.

At 2 P. M. I returned to the Big Tree Grove, five miles from Santa Cruz, entirely in the wilderness.

A long, temporary dining hall, a bar located outside, a summer house built on the stump of a fallen tree comprises the station. These trees belong to the pine family, and when growing on the rocky cliff and gulches of the mountains, measure from a foot and a half to four feet in diameter, and shoot up like an arrow from 100 to 150 feet high. But when it finds a deep and more genial soil, it never stops growing until some convulsion of nature sweeps it off, and when once gone it never returns; as the fossil remains indicate in Alaska and Northern Europe, and the petrified forest on the mountain near Calistogo, hereinafter spoken of. Those groves on the Sierra Nevada and Coast Range Mountains, are all that are left on the face of the globe, and these are fast disappearing. It is one of the most useful woods California has for building purposes, ties and telegraph poles, and will not rot for thousands of years if kept dry. It is brought in long flumes from 30 or 40 miles back on the mountains to the thoroughfares and then conveyed to the different towns and cities.

Now, returning more directly to our subject, the Big Tree Grove is located on the Valley of the San Lorenzo River, five miles from Santa Cruz. The soil, as shown by the railroad cutting, is from 12 to 16 feet deep, and lower in the valley, it is probably 20 or 30 and possibly more.

The trunk has a round symmetrical from throughout its entire length, with a few short limbs. The leaves resemble those of a cedar more than that of a pine. They are about half an inch in length, and resemble a braided silk cord. The roots go directly down into the earth, after forming a swell at the bottom of the tree for a brace. In deep reflection I wandered alone among about forty acres of these giants of the forest, and bowed myself by the river side where the waters gently flowed, and felt a deep sense of the mighty power of a wonder-working God. It is surprising to notice how closely together these trees grow, often two, three or four, connected at the ground will stretch themselves along up side by side, apparently striving to see which should first reach the clouds.

To describe all these trees separately would require much space. I will only mention a few of the most noted.

Fremont's Tree, so called because General Fremont and party camped in it for six weeks whilst exploring the country. It is 300 feet high, and contains a hollow space at the root 16 feet in diameter. The inside was burnt out forming the hollow, and the walls are rather sombre. It was once occupied by a trapper, who had children born in it. A hole was cut through the backside for a stove pipe to pass out, and a natural arched opening about eight feet high in front, which served as a doorway and window.

The ceiling above is lost in darkness. The tree yet lives and flourishes, and doubtless will for ages yet to come. I walked down under the shadow of these monsters, to near the river, to view the remains of an old tannery, constructed by the aforesaid trapper, being the first ever used by white men in California. It consisted of a large red wood being felled, and three sections being hollowed out in trough form for vats, under the shelter of the surrounding forest.

Jumbo standing near General Fremont is of the same size and height. Fillmore is 61 feet in circumference. The three sisters are very large, and starting from the same base of roots, rise 200 feet, then one gracefully bows a little and clasps the other in its branches.

The Giant stands isolated and defiant, and rose to the height of 372 feet; but in its stubbornness to overawe its companions, the Almighty sent his blast and broke off 70 feet of its overshadowing loftiness. It now stands a little over 300 feet, holding equlibrium with its brethren. It is 74 8-12 feet in circumference.

At 6 P. M., I left this awe-inspiring scene and returned to San Francisco, and lodged at the International Hotel.

Monday, October 8th.—I started for Calistogo, 68 miles distant, and the Petrified Forest, 6 miles beyond. Passing Oakland on the Napa Branch, we proceeded up the valley. If there is such a thing, literally, as rivers of wine, they flow through this valley. Truly it is a land of corn and wine. From Oakland the country is very rich and level, extending to the foot hills of the barren mountains on the east.

Long rows of Gum trees ornament the sides of the road, and private grounds along which we passed, vegetable gradens with their rich products, occupy these bottom lands. Turning my attention to San Pablo Bay, on the left, I noticed the marsh was literally covered with gulls. The garden gradually give way to wheat fields, and sacks of grain were piled up by thousand, while the straw was being pressed into bales for shipment. Not a spire of grass or a pound of hay could be seen.

Large herds of cattle were noticed in the Exchange Yards. Mile after mile the stubble fields extend from which the ripened grain was cut, and nothing now of green is seen except the willows that wend their way along the thirsty channel of a dried up stream. Wheat at length gives place to a little corn, and where irrigation is available, the lawns and yards represent a freshness that bespeaks the beauty of Eden's first bloom. Napa City, on Napa River, is a smart town of 5,000 inhabitants, at the head of tide water, connected with San Pablo Bay.

Here we took a steamer and crossed to the other side, and struck the Napa Valley which is about 40 miles long and four miles wide. It is completely hedged in by various spurs of the coast range of mountains, some of which produce a few shrubs and trees, others are utterly naked. The valley has a dark, deep, rich soil, and for the culture of grapes probably is not excelled in the world, producing annually nearly half a million gallons of wine and brandy.

The grape plants in the vinyard are set about eight feet apart. The first and second years they plant a row of corn between each row of grapes, one to two stalks in a hill, having from two to three ears each. In the fall the grape vines are cut back to about 2 1-2 feet of the ground and placed in an upright position. The next fall they are cut back again within six or eight inches of the first cutting, forming a stiff stool or bench.

They are treated in the same way ever after, and no treillage is seen in a vineyard. They flourish without irrigation on account of their depth of root.

This valley from Napa City, to its terminus at Calistogo, 60 miles, may be said to be one continuous line of orchards, gardens, vineyards and wine cellars, all of the richest and most beautiful character.

The road is cut directly through the vineyards, and the vines stand close beside the track on either side, loaded down with rich clusters of delicious grapes, that tempt the palate of the passers by.

I will not particularize all the occupants of these grounds, yet I will mention a few. Oak Knoll, five miles from Napa, is the country residence of Mr. Woodward, of Woodward Gardens, S. F., the farm contains 1,000 acres, 120 of which are devoted to fruit.

Close by is a blackberry ranche of 12 acres, this fruit is also much cultivated. At Youths Ville, 3 1-2 miles farther on, is a large brick wine cellar, surrounded by large vineyards, and a little beyond comes Mason's vineyard of a 100 acres of raisin grapes, dried and packed there. Three miles farther we pass a quicksilver mine on the side of the mountain, and a large wine cellar on the right. Two miles farther, at Bello, is another big wine cellar, surrounded by vineyards also. On again we passed St. Helena, which I will notice on my return. Near by is Kings great vineyard and Orange grove. Leaving St. Helena behind, we soon reached a farm of 500 acres, 115 of which are in a vineyard, and another large wine cellar close by the road.

At Borro, two miles farther, the valley narrows up to two miles, and the vineyards extend back on the hill sides.

Napa Creek, which we have followed all the way, now dwindles down and disappears. Three miles farther we arrived at Calistogo, the end of the road, and end of the valley, being surrounded on three sides by mountains, and nestling under their shadow. This is a quiet little town of 500 inhabitants, also a noted watering place. The Calistogo Etna Boiling Springs are located here, visited by invalids and tourists, for health and pleasure.

Arriving about midday I hasted at once to the springs which were near by, and on entering the grounds I read a sign, "Cook for Yourselves." Pleased with the novel idea of cooking food in nature's boiling cauldron, I stood for a few moments by it, in awe stricken wonder, and watched its ebullitions, which were not violent, but such as we witness when a kettle of water commences to boil, with a dense steam arising from its surface.

Scarcely believing my own vision, I thurst my hand into it and burnt my finger. It has a temperature of 212°. Much has been done to ornament the grounds. About a dozen dwellings have been erected for the use of invalids and tourists, with large palmetto trees lining the walks in front. In the rear is a knob containing about five acres, in a circular form, rising directly from the surrounding plain one hundred feet, with a fountain located on the summit. Between the fountain and the base are many large cactus growing, and here and there the famous century plant are located, covering a surface of 20 or 30 feet circumference. Two of the same have blossomed, the flower stems are four feet in circumference at the base, and rising in the air from 16 to 20 feet, then branching out with a fine show of flowers at the top.

Wild oats are to be seen here as well as in many other parts of California. Mount St. Helena, an extinct volcano now looms up before us 3,243 feet high, and is difficult of access. The whole country bears evidence of volcanic action.

At 1 P. M., I took the stage for the Petrified Forest on the western range of mountains. A gentlemen and three ladies arriving at the same time.

A cottage and cabinet of fossil remains stood near the road, with a young German in attendance, who was totally devoid of every shadow of geological or scientific information. He received fifty cents each for admission, went around and showed us where the trees lay, then left us to study nature, and reason for ourselves. The ground on which the forest lies comprises 40 acres of a former plateau, with the mountain peaks surrounding it, rising 500 feet above. On the western rim of this plateau the land breaks off in a more gradual descent.

Cropping out around this rim are seen these sleeping monsters of the days of yore, being broken off across this rim and the op portions either buried in the debris below or decayed away. The trunks extend back on the plateau being buried in volcanic ashes and lava.

They are shown by excavation being carried back 60 or 80 feet, until the ashes over them are 10 to 15 feet in thickness. Were they wholly unearthed, doubtless they would represent trees of the red wood variety of 400 or 500 feet in length. The largest trunk yet brought to view is 33 feet in circumference and 80 feet to where it broke over the precipice.

Counting the rings that encircle this petrified giant, I estimated it to have been 3,000 years old when it was laid down to sleep, and the untold millions of ages that have since passed, no tongue can tell. They are broken up into sections from three to twenty feet in length, and as direct across as though cut with a saw.

Over the plateau where these monarchs once flourished in the "long ago," now is nothing but a barren waste of volcanic ashes and lava, with here and there a scattering shrub, and not a tree of red wood within a hundred miles.

No one, as far as I can learn, has undertaken to explain this wonderful phenomenon. And, if I undertake to investigate it from practical observation, I shall subjugate myself to ridicule by the scientist, which I must forego, and relate it as nature presents it to my understanding.

The germinating period of these trees we can not reach, yet circumstances would point it back as far as the biblical creation. All the perfect record we have are the rings that encircle them, which is from 3,000 to 5,000, indicating that number of years.

After that period had pacifically passed, there was a mighty upheaving of nature in consequence of the internal fires that struggled within, and the forest was all thrown down. The trees lie in parallel lines, all fallen in the same direction, plainly showing that the earth being raised up on one side, pitched them all in an opposite direction.

Mount St. Helena broke out at the same time, giving vent to the internal burning; the ashes and lava falling back and burying the forest ten or twenty feet deep as it lies there to-day. It could not rot, and as ages passed away it at length became solid stone.

Having finished my investigations, I retraced my journey to Calistogo, passing on the way large beds of ashes and lava that had run down from the extinct volcano in prehistoric ages, and formed foot hills to the mountain.

Although the volcano of St. Helena has become extinct, yet that ocean of melted lava within still heats up the waters that are sent out in the boiling springs, which hold no perceptible mineral in solution.

On reaching the town I purchased some eggs and other articles, and immediately repaired to the Hot Spring to do my cooking. I boiled the eggs finely, and steeped the tea in the best manner, then sat down and enjoyed a repast directly from the hand of nature. I lingered around this boiling fountain in contemplation till darkness closed the scene, adoring that "Power whose ways are mysterious and past finding out." Staid at the Spring Hotel.

Tuesday, October 9th.—I purchased a return ticket, paid $2.70, came as far as St. Helena on the early train and got off.

St. Helena is a terrestrial paradise, with a population of 1,200; among whom are many angelic beings, whose friendship, freedom and good will, manifest to strangers, make them at once forget they are strangers in a strange land, and feel themselves at home, surrounded by the blessings of friendship, love and peace.

I passed through the business portion of the town to the west side and struck a beautiful street, with neatly finished residences, surrounded by vines, trees, fruits and flowers. I could not pass all these beauties by. Entering a yard, the lady gave me a hearty welcome and the freedom of the grounds, filled my hands with figs, a sack with grapes, and my heart with gratitude. I bestowed my blessing upon her and departed. A little farther on I noticed rose bushes trained up like shrubs or trees, and a large fig tree with branches bowed to the earth with ripened fruit, while lovely cypress trees ornamented the foreground.

Fascinated by the sight, my footsteps led me to the door where a lady and her daughter were standing under the shadowing branches of a fig tree, from which I picked and ate a few directly from the branches. The lady then sent her amiable daughter on the lawn to show me the different fruits and flowers, and also to gather some almonds, which I retain for the donor's sake, whose smiling face I never more expect to see.

A mile or two farther on I noticed a beautiful cottage embowered in trees, fruits and shrubs, with vineyards on the surroundings and treillaged walks amid the lawns. I could not pass it by, but entered there.

The same free, open-heartedness was at once expressed, and I was made welcome to all I desired of everything my eyes could rest upon. I wandered about the vineyard in wonder and astonishment, at beholding the loads of luscious fruit those bushes bore, the clusters resting one upon the other.

Passing along up I came to Beninger Bro's Wine Cellar. Mr. Beninger showed me the cellar which was hewn out under the mountain, through a soft, chalky rock substance, supposed to be composed of volcanic ashes that once fell from the crater of St. Helena in bygone ages. The main tunnel of the cellar runs back 100 feet, then branches to the right and left forming a cross. The arch overhead is of the same material as the sides, all self-supporting. All were filled with immense tierces of wine, containing 1,000 gallons each.

Next he showed the crusher, the pulp from which passed into a hopper that led through the floor to the presses below. Claret, however, is fermented on the skins, the other varieties are fermented in the casks with a sack of sand over the bung. He said 20 tons of grapes had been raised per acre, on the valley, yet five tons might be considered a fair yield on the higher lands. No fertilizers are used. He gave me a glass of wine, and with friendship we parted. Enchanted by the fascinating scenes I was passing by, unconsciously I had retrograded two or three miles, and was opposite of Krug Station in the valley below. I turned directly to the right and made my way down through a vineyard that really seemed to groan under the weight of fruit, to the station, where is located another wine cellar.

Mr. Charles Krug, proprietor, sat by a fountain overshadowed by willows, smoking a cigar. He said to me, go about the flower grounds, fruit gardens and wine buildings with perfect freedom, where you choose, and when satisfied, come to me and I will impart such information as you desire.

I first trod the isles of the beautiful flower grounds, then entered the fruit garden, where a fig-tree had broken under its load of fruit. Quinces were of enormous size. The rich and luscious peaches, plums and pears would have satisfied the most sanguine epicure.

A wagon load of grapes in boxes, containing about 50 pounds each, stood at the elevator, were gradually emptied on and carried to the crusher above, which separated the stems from the pulp.

Here I again met the Hon. Mr. Krug. He said to me, "come, now, have a glass of claret;" after which he wrote the following statistics in my book :

Charles Krug, of Krug's Station, has 225 acres of vineyard. Made 274,000 gallons of wine in 1882.

The wine cellar is 160 by 130 feet, and has a capacity of 500,000 gallons. I have been in the place 23 years.

Feeling a deep sense of gratitude and friendship for Mr. Krug, I shook hands and invoked the benediction: "May the Lord ever bless the kind citizens of St. Helena, as they have this day blessed me."

The railroad track being cut directly through the vineyards, I took its course back to the station where I got off in the morning. Meeting on my way Mr. G. R. Warrel near his vineyard, he took me out among the fruit, told me of the adapting certain varieties, to certain purposes. He then said he and Mr. Ward had 24 acres which produced 207 tons last year. He picked some of the different varieties, filled a small sack for me, saying I was welcome to all I could carry away. As strangers we met, and friendship glowed—we parted, expect to meet no more.

At 3.20 p. m. I went on board the cars and started for San Francisco with a heart overflowing with gratitude to the kind people, and my basket overflowing with the choicest fruits of the land. Arrived at International Hotel, San Francisco, 8 p. m. As I was walking down Kearney street my attention was arrested by a crowd gathered around a sign in the middle of the street, on which I read, "Salvation Army Meeting. Jesus, the only Saviour." I stopped, looked and listened, to see and hear the medley that was at that moment transpiring within sight and hearing. Singing and exhortation, band playing before the theater, instrumental music flowing from beer saloons on every hand, connected with dancing and waltzing. Electric machines and athletics were being performed. Target shooting in the shooting galleries, mercantile trade and traffic in the shops, auction rooms with shout and laugh, such is the miscellany of this busy street.

Tuesday, October 9th, I retired at 11 P. M. and soon fell asleep. At 1.05 A. M. a terrible rumbling and roaring was heard, the house rocked to and fro like a cradle. Suddenly awaking, I jumped to the floor to hear patting of feet all over the house, and from every ones' lips the same words, "earthquake." Such things are common here, and soon all was still again.

Wednesday, October 10, 1883, I bade adieu to San Francisco, and started for home, over the Southern Pacific route, and its connections through Los Angeles, Yuma, Deming, Elpaso, Santa Fe, Las Vegas, Topeka, Kansas City, St. Louis, Indianapolis, Cleveland and Niagara Falls to Utica.

Our course first led north along San Pablo Bay to Vallejio, then turned southeast on the San Pablo Railroad to Lathrop, through one continuous line of wheat fields, where millions of bushels in sacks lay about the stations awaiting shipment. Here we took dinner. From this station tourists go ten miles north to Stockton, 20 east to Milton, then by stage 40 miles to Calaveras Big trees—fare $20. Leaving Lathrop, we took a southeast course, 350 miles, passing up the Great San Joaquin Valley. This valley alone is larger than many kingdoms of the old world, being 200 miles in length, and 30 in width, embracing 6,000,000 acres of arid lands, and 1,000,000 more of tuiles (marsh land, covered with bulrushes,) richest in the world when reclaimed. An account of the grain and stock raised in this valley would appear fabulous.

Fifty-five miles from Lathrop brought us to Merced, an important town, population, 3,000. The county of Merced in 1876 produced 4½ millions bushels of wheat, besides rye, corn, peas, beans, potatoes, alfalfa, (a species of clover,) tobacco, cotton and other crops. These arid lands in the state of nature, produce little or nothing, but by the hardy nerve of the enterprising eastern man, a grand and extensive system of irrigation has been brought into requisition, and conveying water over all the country.

The San Joaquin and King's River Canal is 100 miles long, 68 feet wide, and six feet deep. The irrigating ditches fed from this alone, would manure thousands of miles.

The travel for the Yosemite formerly took stages here, but now they generally take the stage at Madeira, 33 miles south, over a better road and shorter route, passing through Mariposa Big Tree Grove. The stage fare is the same either way, being $45.00.

Madeira is a lively little place of 300 inhabitants, and their enterprise is seen far back into the mountains. They have a V flume 53 miles long, through which large quantities of lumber are floated down from the saw mills back on the mountains. Twelve miles from Madeira we crossed the San Joaquin River at Sycamore, 200 miles from San Francisco, and left the valley behind. Yet the country is still flat and little cultivated to Fresno, 10 miles, representing a cemetery of round mounds, from two to five feet high. What they contain deponent saith not.

The soil about Fresno inclines to clay, producing, if irrigated, if not, it is like faith without works, yielding nothing.

The high peaks of the Sierra, are seen on the left, covered with snow the year round. Thirty-five miles from the San Joaquin River, we crossed the Kings River, all the channels between these are dry, water being raised by wind-mills for irrigation, without which not a kernel of any thing will grow. Kings Valley is about 40 miles wide, occupied almost exclusively for sheep ranches. At Goshen we struck the Southern Pacific Railroad, 241 miles from San Francisco. The several divisions of road thus far passed over, are operated by the Central Pacific Railroad.

The southern road when completed to San Francisco will pass some miles west of the line we came over; where the land is said to produce five crops of alfalfa a year, and pumpkins eight feet in circumference. All the land about Goshen, Tulare and Tulare Lake is rich beyond description, and will produce any kind of vegetable or plant that is put in the ground, by irrigation, without which not a seed will grow.

A gentleman on the cars said to me, these rich and fertile lands are worth a dollar an acre, and water is worth forty dollars. No timber is seen except what is planted. He farther stated that alfalfa was known to root down twenty feet, and from three to four crops in a year could be cut and sold at $10 per ton.

Ten miles farther we reached a barren section at Tipton, and pass beyond the Tulare Lake, which is but thirty miles long and twenty-five wide.

This uncultivated waste continues fifty-two miles without a tree, shrub or plant, passing over many dry runs and broad irrigating ditches, but not a drop of water could be seen until arriving at Kern River, which we crossed on a long trestle bridge, the banks being lined with green willow.

At Buena Vista, forty miles away, large quantities of oil are found in holes and ditches in the earth.

On striking the Kern Valley there is a sudden transition from barren waste to the richest and most productive lands on the globe. This valley is very broad and extends to the base of the Sierras.

The soil is almost wholly composed of sedimentary deposits, washed down from the mountains in long ages past. In no part of California, or as far as we know, on the earth, is farming carried on so extensively as on these rich bottom lands. An account of the productions seem so wonderful that I dare not relate them only as statistics give them to me.

Irrigation is very extensive. One canal is 40 miles in length, 275 feet wide, and eight feet deep. Besides the canals, there are many wells and windmills.

Mr H. L. Livermore, has one ranche, containing 7,000 acres, on which are two flowing artesian wells, one 300 feet deep. From these wells the water rises 12 feet above the surface, and discharges over 80,000 gallons per day. On the ranche is 150 miles of irrigating ditches—3,000 acres of the farm are in alfalfa, from which four to six crops a year are cut. He has another ranche on which are 500 acres in alfalfa and 3,000 in wheat and barley. These ranches are stocked with 8,000 sheep, 4,000 stock cattle, 300 cows, 350 horses, 100 oxen, 70 mules, and 1,500 hogs. He has a plow, the largest in the world, weighing over a ton, drawn by 80 oxen, cutting a furrow five feet wide, and three feet deep, moving eight miles a day. Another called Sampson, used for cutting ditches, drawn by 40 mules.

Mr. Livermore's neighbor has 40,000 sheep, 2,000 acres of alfalfa, raises also 60,000 bushels of grain. A third, for I will tell of no others, has 16,000 sheep and raised in 1877 4,200 tons of pumpkins and sweet potatoes. Some of the former weighing 210 pounds each, and the latter 15 1-2 pounds. Yet with all their wealth, they are said not to be happy. We have now passed over 304 miles of entirely level country to Sumner, where we begin to climb the foot hills of the Sierras, with an up grade of 20 miles, we come directly to the frowning cliffs of the mountains at Caliente, and enter a deep gorge and are hid from the world, and begin to climb the mountain in earnest. We have now 25 miles to travel to reach the summit; with an up grade of over 100 feet to the mile, and within the distance will pass through 17 tunnels, aggregating 7,683 feet, and then "Over the Loop" which is considered one of the greatest feats of engineering skill ever accomplished. The road passes under a high peak, shoots off, loops around, returning farther up the mountain, looping back, still rising, and making another return, and looping around a second time, shoots up the mountain, crossing over the towering height that we had so lately passed under, and when eight miles from Caliente, we had made but one mile of progress up the steep ascent, and could look down and see the town lying at our feet.

On climbing up this rugged eminence, the scenery is constantly changing, around rocky points, over high embankments, through deep cuts, and tunnel after tunnel, then deep ravines that grow deeper still at every turn until they become a fearful gorge. Climbing, turning and twisting, to gain altitude until we arrived at a tunnel, and where we looked down from a dizzy height into an awful, fearful chasm; yet we passed on safely upwards, turning first to the right and then to the left, passing tunnels from twelve to seventeen in quick succession, brought us to Tehachapi Summit, the highest point on the road, 3,964 feet above the sea, on a broad plateau of thousands of acres, near the bed of a dry lake where salt can be shoveled up.

Unfortunately this scenery was passed through in the night, yet it could not be lost. The atmosphere was clear, the stars shone brightly and I took a station on the rear platform which I held possession of till 2 o'clock in the morning. All the windings and turnings were gracefully made, it was amusing to fix my eyes on a certain constellation that appeared in front, and hold my attention there, while it gradually appeared to move around and was at length seen in the rear, but still moving on, it appeared in front again. From the summit we had a down grade, 20 miles to Majova on the desert. Majova is a shipping point to the mines east of the Sierras, 150 miles distant, and 350 teams are employed in freight hauling. From Majova, we crossed 36 miles of uninhabited desert, where but little was seen except rat-tail cactus, which brought us to the foot of Soledad Mountain, which we then passed over at an altitude of 3,211 feet, which we arose and descended again in the distance of ten miles. In this mountain is the Robbers' Roost, with wall 2,000 feet high. It was the rendezvous of Vanques' Robber Band, who was hung in St. Joe, 1875. Five others were taken from a jail and hung—no questions.

Advancing twelve miles more, the spurs of the mountain again crossed our track, and we this time passed under them, coming out at Lang, Thursday morning, October 11th.

What a dismal picture dawned upon us. Nothing but barren mountains and a little sage bush could be seen. Passing over thirteen miles of this desolation, we arrived at New Hall Valley, where wheat again appeared and evergreen oaks were scattered about the fields. Mr. New Hall owns 50,000 acres of land, and herds of stock and droves of horses. This is a great stage centre also. Looking forward we beheld a hog's-back ridge of the San Fernando Mountains rising 3,000 feet high directly before us, and no possible way of getting over them. We cast one shudder, and before the second thought could arise we were plunged into total darkness in a tunnel 6,967 feet long. Emerging from the tunnel, we struck the rich valley of San Fernando, not yet brought into cultivation; bearing its native cactus and sage bush.

At Andrews are several oil wells, said to be very rich. The country now opens out like a broad sea, and a few miles more brought us to Los Angeles at 8 A. M.

This is an old Mexican town, situate on the Los Angeles River, in a broad, expansive valley, 470 miles southeast of San Francisco. It was settled in 1771, and many of the old adobe buildings still remain that were erected more than a hundred years ago. Their peculiar appearance and antiquated construction, claimed my first attention. The brick of which they are built are made of mortar mixed with straw, twenty-four inches long, fifteen wide, and four inches thick, dried in the sun, the same as ancient Egyptian brick. The buildings are but one story high, and occupied now by the Chinese. They are only found on one side of the city, the residue being built up in modern and magnificent style. Population 16,000. The shops of the railroad company are the chief manufactures. It is a railroad centre and has a great trade. The city is completely embowered in foliage with vineyards on every hand. Being laid out on such an expansive plan that every man has a fruit orchard of his own, and the fruits are so numerous we can not mention them all, yet we noticed oranges, lemons, limes, pomegranates, figs, apples, pears, plums, cherries, peaches, almonds, walnuts, and an infinite variety of smaller fruits, while evergreens have no end—palms, bananas, Italian and Monterey, cypress, live oak, eucalyptus, and that most lovely and beautiful of all trees, the pepper. Flowers and roses ornament the yards and lawns the year round. It is just one continued garden and vineyard, laden and bowed down with the richest and most luscious fruits—a paradise

D

on earth—a second Eden. The same scene of luxury, loveliness, fertility and beauty, extends to the south and east as far as the eye can reach.

Why, O why, could not mother Eve have lingered longer here?

My friend and former neighbor, A. A. Sanders, found me soon after entering the city, and gave me a hearty greeting—took me to his house, a snug little home embowered in trees, and after dinner hired a livery, took his wife and daughter in company with me on a ride to Pasadena, (Key of the Valley), seven miles northeast of Los Angeles. Only seven years ago this place was occupied solely by Garfias and family, a Spaniard, who owned the ranche.

A company of men from Indiana purchased the tract, divided and sub-divided it into thirty 15 and 7½ acre lots, which were at once taken by enterprising men of means, and a town, in beauty and loveliness, arose at once, as by magic from the earth, peopled with citizens of the highest class.

They have an abundance of water that is brought forty miles, and every tree and shrub is irrigated. Not a weed or spire of grass can be seen.

The neat and stately mansions, the orange, lemon and apple orchards, trees and vines that cluster around every dwelling, laden with their first fruits, give the place a fascinating charm, and we can scarcely realize that earth can be made so beautiful. The naked grounds out of town are covered with little mounds, having a hole in the top—habitations of ground squirrels. The dear little fellows stood on their hind feet erect looking at us as we passed by. Beautiful and cunning as they appear, poison is manufactured for their destruction. Their burrows are closely guarded by owls without, and rattlesnakes within. Seeing one standing some way off, Mr. Sanders sent a portion of cold lead after him to enquire into his business. It reached the ground under him, but did not fully communicate its message. His lordship turned around facing us, and made three graceful bows, then ejaculated, "Whoo ho, who hooe!" Mr. Sanders sent a second messenger that whispered in his ear danger, he then changed base.

Returning to the city, I took rooms at the Southern Hotel.

Friday, October 12, 1883.—I started for Washington Gardens, in the city, four miles distant, passing orange groves and gardens all the way. In my walk I stopped at Philip Felthamsar's, corner of 12th and Olive streets; said he paid $10,000 for three and one-half acres less than a year ago, and had now refused $25,000. The soil is a dark, sedimentary substance, four feet deep, producing fabulously; said he raised peaches twelve inches in circumference, weighing one pound each. English walnuts eight bushels to a tree. Apricots sell at $2 per hundred weight. He granted me the liberty of the grounds. I picked and ate what oranges and white figs I desired, (the white figs are best). Bananas are growing also. A neighbor showed me a sack containing 60 pounds of walnuts that he gathered from a tree 10 years old.

I passed on to the Washington Gardens, introduced myself to Mr. D. V. Waldron, proprietor. He cordially received me as a stranger and friend, and very generously granted me perfect freedom to all the grounds, 35 acres, and all the oranges, apples and fruit I wished to eat or take away. Inside the gate a rose tree, 18 inches in circumference, and a red wood from Calaveras' grove first met my eye, then a spacious grape arbor, with the most delicious clusters hanging thickly overhead and pendant all around. Fig trees bowing to the ground, each one forming a bower of its own. In the rear of the building were bowers of roses, enlivened by the song of mocking birds that are so tame as to light on the children's heads, and sometimes call people from different parts of the grounds by imitating a signal whistle. The beautiful pepper trees stood around a fountain, with their boughs drooping and resting on the earth. The leaf of the tree is a perfect fern. The fruit hangs in shreds, attached to a long stem, and resembles pepper. The apple and pear trees were breaking under their load of fruit, while apples, pears and oranges lay scattered all over the ground besides. I picked up a fruit of the lemon specie, fifteen inches in circumference. Mr. Waldron said he had shipped seven car loads of oranges from his trees already, and some men were still picking and boxing. I was permitted to climb the ladder to the top of an orange tree and pick some fruit for that purpose. Returning to the office with what fruit I desired, Mr. Waldron then took a tape and stepped on the walk to measure an eucalyptus tree that was but seven years from the seed. It measured five feet in circumference at the ground, and rising straight as a line eighty feet in the air. I now parted with my friend Mr. Waldron, and returned back to the more business portion of the city.

On my way thither I saw a four horse team standing that had just brought in 17 large casks full of grapes to a Mexican wine press. They were emptied into two square vats inclining towards a tub. Fourteen Mexicans, some barefoot, others with rubbers on, immediately stepped in and "trod the wine press," but not alone, the pulp running off into the tub. In the afternoon I went to the Agricultural Fair, where they had a baby show that afternoon, and a race course a little out of town.

On my return, I passed the oldest orange grove in Los Angeles, with trees 20 or 30 feet high and a foot through at the ground. On this second return, I met friend Sanders again who took me on a high eminence and showed me all the town, river and valley, at once, embowered in everlasting green, and cypress adornings. I returned to the Southern Hotel for the night.

———

On Saturday morning October 13, when about to depart, my friend, A. A. Sanders, Captain 2nd Battalion Light Artillery, K. S. M., and Chief of Ordnance on Governor St. John's staff, gave me the parting hand at the depot, and I turned my face eastward. From Los Angeles we had a gentle up grade 80 miles.

Just beyond the city bounds we passed close by the old San Gabriel Mission Church. It is built of adobe, and is in a dilapidated state, having stood there 100 years. There are five bells to be seen hanging in the steeple representing a cross.

The San Gabriel mission is down on the San Gabriel river, founded in 1771, being the first one located of the 21 in California. These missionary settlements in the wilderness were all sent out from the City of Mexico, by the College of San Fernando, and were all of the order of Franciscan Friars. The orange orchards were the first planted in California, now very large, yet produce the best of fruit. Two miles from the station is L. J. Roses' orange grove, containing 500 acres, planted by General Stoneman.

The Pad Cactus grows in great abundance in plats, here and there, to a height of ten feet. The fruit has a pleasant flavor, used chiefly by the natives. San Gabriel Wine Company have a large establishment a little farther east, and at Pomona is a reservoir containing 3,000,000 gallons of water supplied by artesian wells.

The country thus far seems to be given to agriculture and sheep culture, corn, wheat, rye, oats and barley, are extensively raised; and many hogs are fed about Monte Spear Pomona. On a broad uncultivated valley where nothing grew, we came up to a wrecked train of merchandise. It was the most complete mass of chaos my eyes ever beheld. A track was soon laid around it, and we passed on. The wreck was caused by an axle burning off.

Colton is 57 miles from Los Angeles at the foot of the San Bernando mountains. River Side Colony is a little south of the track, comprises 8,000 acres of fine land spread over with irrigating ditches. A resident occupying a seat with me gave a glowing account of its thriving condition.

San Bernando is four miles northeast of the station; settled in 1847, by Josephite Mormons, at the same time that Salt Lake City was settled by Brighamites. It is laid out in the same manner as Salt Lake City, and all other Mormon towns, with water coursing down its streets, and embowered in trees, fruits and flowers. Population 6,000. The valley contains 36,000 acres of the finest lands, on which are raised two crops a year, first 50 bushels of barley, then 60 of corn to the acre, and 5 crops of alfalfa.

At Colton, 57 miles from Los Angeles, a second engine was attached to our train to help us up the mountain on a grade of near 100 feet to the mile, to San Gorgonia on the summit, a distance of 23 miles. The first 15 miles of our course was up a narrow canon where nothing of life can be seen but a few sheep, then striking Eleasco, a narrow ravine, 1-4 of a mile wide, we found a soil from six to twelve feet deep. Here are immense quantities of peaches raised and a few grapes.

The ravine becomes more and more narrow until at last it closes into a gorge, where we loose sight of California fruitfulness. Like Lot's wife, we could not help looking back and breath farewell, to all your loveliness and beauty, farewell! and if it must be forever, "Still, forever fare thee well!"

We continued up the gorge with naked mountains on either side shooting up in all imaginary forms, and not a vestige of green could be seen until we arrived at San Gorgonia on the summit. From here we had 28 miles of down grade winding around these naked cliffs, to reach Seven Palms at the foot of the mountain on the east side. The water here is good, and no more is found till we reach the Colorado River at Yuma 137 miles, except such as is brought from the mountains in pipes to the stations.

From Seven Palms to Indio, 21 miles, (after leaving the valley, where are a few cactus and low prickly palms,) the mountains approach near on both sides rising directly from the sandy desert in utter nakedness. Not a specie of any kind of vegetation is to be seen, and the valley is as destitute as the mountains, presenting one continuous scene of sandy desolation every where, until Indio is reached, a little oasis in the desert, around the station of one house only, where we got dinner by paying a dollar. After leaving this station a singular phenomenon presents itself to view. The water washed shore of an extinct sea is plainly marked by the lines of shell and water washed pebbles that encircle it. We have now 60 miles travel to cross this basin and at times are 266 feet below the level of the sea. For about 15 miles from Indio, rat-tail cactus, musquite, and shrub palms cover the surface, then we strike a salt region that extends 45 miles, until we emerge from the basin through which not a specie of vegetation is to be seen, and silent desolation reigns supreme. This basin is entirely dry except 25 square miles of salt, mud springs, which boil like so many cauldrons of soap. After leaving this depression, grease wood and sage again appear, until the winding course of the Colorado is marked by its green willows and arrived at Yuma, in Arizona, on the Colorado River, 730 miles from San Francisco, at 8 P. M., then paid a dollar for lodging and retired.

The city contains a population of 1,500, mostly Spanish Mexicans and Indians. Aside from the railroad shop and buildings, it is entirely built of adobe, (sun dried brick,) and mud huts, of only one story, having a few small windows. The walls are from two to four feet thick. They have but one roof, and that is nearly flat, formed by a layer of poles covered with willows, and two feet of dirt put on top of it. They all have verandas projecting from 10 to 20 feet, to shield them from the scorching sun, covered in the same way. The mud houses are built by setting four crotches in the ground, for the four corners, then laying poles in these to support a roof, which is made of dirt as before spoken of. The side walls are made by setting willow poles close together, one end in the ground, and the other attached to the supporting horizontal pole above, while the cracks between are plastered up with mud. The doorways serve as windows. They often sleep on the roofs of their houses, covered by nature's veil—darkness.

Frost and snow are unknown.

Each house has a rear yard, made of poles set in the ground, close together, the tops running unequal, in a jagged form, from four to twelve feet high. Four feet from the ground they are all fastened to horizontal poles by rawhides. Not a blade of grass, or vestige of vegetation of any kind is seen about their dwellings, and no cultivated fields are in the neighborhood nearer than the Indian Reservation on the Colorado River, which is annually flooded by the river as Egypt is by the Nile. It then produces corn, melons and pumpkins.

At Yuma the river bottom is merely covered by willows.

The river rises in Idaho, passes through the Grand Canon, with walls 3,500 feet high, watering eight States in its course, and empties into the Gulf of California. The Indians from the Reservation are daily seen walking or sitting about the streets of Yuma, with painted faces in barbarous style. Some of them have a heavy scarf of beads around the neck, and hair curled in ringlets about the shoulders. Their dresses are nature's covering, with the exception of a knit jacket about the stomach, a belt around the hips, with a long red scarf attached, adjusted in Father Adam's fig leaf apron style, attached to the belt behind and hanging to the ground. They are friendly, notwithstanding their appearance.

Fort Yuma is abandoned, and the Quartermaster's Department is used only as a United States Signal Station. Mercury to-day 90½.

————

Sunday, October 14th, I visited the deserted convent, it did not succeed as a school and was abandoned. The cemetery also claimed my attention, which is merely a sandy spot with a few sticks standing to mark the graves, and occasionally a board bearing a Spanish inscription.

The inhabitants are chiefly Catholics, and have the only place of worship in the town. They are very zealous in their belief and manifest more humility and penitence than churches in more popular places. The edifice is built of adobe, yet being superior to others in having a floor, while many have only nature's footing, earth. A row of slips was on either side, an aisle through the center, organ and altar in the rear. I was first in the church. All the arrivals went through the usual ceremonies at the fount, bowing to the Virgin and before the Cross. Yet their disposal about the house was rather peculiar. A young and cleanly dressed lady came in and sat directly on the floor, which in course of the gathering was followed by some others. Some fell upon their knees and remained there during a portion of the service. One old man continued to count his beads, while still another stood close behind a pilaster with his face to the wall. A great number stood on the floor about the door blessing themselves with their motions which were quicker than they could repeat the words, " Father, Son and Holy Ghost." As soon as the priest entered the house, the candles were lighted. Singing with music from the organ, carried out the sentiment of the priest's prayer. An attendant swung to and fro a burning lamp of incense. After the discourse, a collection was taken up, during which time music was again performed on the organ, with singing. The ceremonies were all solemn, but being in Spanish, I understood not a word.

Night drew her mantle around, and as but one train a day passed over the road, I was forced to take it at 8 P. M. the same time I got off the night before.

The Gila River is 300 miles long, flowing from the east and uniting with the Colorado River at Yuma. Our course followed up this river for the first 20 miles. The willows on its banks were occasionally seen. We then struck directly out into the vast expansive Gila Desert, and for a hundred miles there is not a habitation, except the railroad buildings to be seen. Neither is there on all this desert, a bird, beast or living thing, except it be a few woodpeckers or owls, and reptiles on which they feed, and I saw none of those. In the distance all the way on the right and left, sombre, bare and naked mountains, raise their rocky desolate heads, as monuments of a forsaken land. No vegetation grows, not a stream passes, and no water is to be had on the railroad for 100 miles, except what is brought on the cars from the Colorado River at Yuma. On this desert 104½ miles east of Yuma, is a track station where two men reside to look after the safety of the road, and is called Painted Rock; named from the painted rocks in its vicinity, which cover about an acre of land, and are fifty feet high, on which are deeply carved in the surface, in Egyptian style, rude representations of men, animals, birds, reptiles and all manner of things real and imaginary. This being the work of a prehistoric age, I much desired to witness it; and being told at Yuma it had oft been seen two and one half miles from the station, I resolved to stop there, although it would be in the night, and on the desert.

The conductor kindly stopped the train and let me off, saying the trackman should flag the next night at the same time, and I could go on again. A monster dog disputed my way to the house and I remained outside till daylight, then going to the door, I found two burly Irishmen cooking their breakfast.

I told them I desired a litte information respecting the locality of Painted Rock, from which the station took its name, and also the conductor said, they should flag for me the next night and I could go on again. I farther remarked, I was willing to pay them for so doing. The leading character very crustily replied, "we know nothing about Painted Rock—all the rocks are painted here. This is not a flag station, and I have no orders to flag for any thing but section purposes, and I will flag for no one." I then begged for liberty to read a few lines of history to enlighten his mind on the subject of the wonderful scene I was in search of. He replied: "No, no; we will hear nothing about it."

A hand car stood on the track and two Chinamen by it. They boarded the vehicle and wheeled away, saying they were going a mile or two east. Astonished and amazed, I looked around and found myself and the dog in supreme power of the station. But of what avail is a man's sovereignty on a desert alone?

I went out on the desert, but destitute of a guide or the least information, returned again. What could I do? I had no hope of getting on board if I waited until night when the next train would pass, while 16 miles lay before me to Gila Bend, the nearest station, and desert all the way without a drop of water; having 90° of heat pouring down upon my head. I resolved to stem the tide, took off my coat, pressed it in my sachel with my books, papers and lunch making about 50 pounds; swinging it on my back, and set my face eastward.

Every half mile I sat down to rest, and would occasionally eat an orange to allay my thirst. Advancing four miles, which seemed to be four times that distance, I met the hand-car returning. I asked for some water. The boss replied, " I will give any man water, but will give nothing else, neither will I flag for any one." I afterwards learned that the statute required all trains if flagged to stop and give water to wanderers on the desert. This favor he durst not refuse. The Chinamen then asked me if I would have some tea. I drank some and filled a little pail holding about a pint, which was all I had for the residue of the day and twelve miles travel. I blessed those Chinamen, although called heathen—I bless them still. I drank very sparingly of my tea until it was gone, then returning the pail to my sachel, found that butter in another small pail had melted down to oil.

When my apples and oranges were gone I had nothing to allay my thirst; so I kept some dry tea in my mouth to draw moisture to my lips.

Gila Bend is named from a bend in the river, where I arrived just at dark, and felt as though the moisture from my frame was nearly all exhausted; yet thankful to my Heavenly Father for the preservation of my strength to reach that place in safety. I drank more than two quarts of hot tea, as fast as it could be steeped, with a little water also, before my thirst could be allayed.

I remained at Gila Bend until 2.30 in the morning, when I got on the next train and reported to the conductor who, in a little time, introduced me to the superintendent who inquired into the conduct of the track man, then said : " we want no such men in our employ—we want men who know something, and when you return this way again, probably you will not find him there."

The Gila Desert is also called the Majova Desert, on which we continued until 77 miles from Painted Rock, when we arrived at Cassa Grande at four o'clock Tuesday morning, October 16.

Undismayed by my late defeat, I now resolved to visit the pre-historic ruins of Casse Grande, sixteen miles north of the station, on the edge of the desert twelve miles from Gila river. No other ruins in Arizona are so well preserved. These remain the same as they were 300 years ago, when the Jesuit Fathers first discovered them.

And even at that early date, there was not so much as a shadow of tradition among the natives, that led to any information respecting who built these works; where the people came from; or whither they went; and nothing has been learned since. Their tools of metal, (if any they had), with which they cut and carved the stone, have long ages past been eaten up with rust, and turned back to dust; while nothing now remains to tell their tale save the hieroglyphics on the Painted Rocks, and other places, which no man can read. The Papago Indians now occupy the country. I paid $5 stage fare, and at seven A. M. started for the ruins. Our course led directly out on to the open desert; after traveling a few miles we crossed the dry, sandy bed of a lake, spread out as smooth as a canvas.

Passing still farther on we reached the Cacti grounds, still on the Gila Desert, where the cactus rear their heads like mighty specters far and near all over the plains. They are as round as a barrel, and twice as large, rising from twenty to sixty feet in the air. They are grooved in straight lines from top to bottom, three inches apart. They are the Boss Cacti, the largest in the world. The whole surface is covered with sharp thorns two inches long, defying approach; yet the woodpecker bores a few holes in them to rear its young. The fruit grows directly on the top, completely spreading over all the surface, and is much prized by the natives. We traveled twelve miles on this plain, which is entirely level; then stopping to change horses where is merely an adobe grog shop, and a miserable apology for stables. Four miles farther we approached a section scattered over with musquite, a crooked shrub producing a fruit in a pod, resembling a bean, yet much smaller. It is gathered in large quantities for food by the natives. Standing here surrounded by this crooked, scraggly, shrubby mass, rearing high her lonely head, is Cassa Grande, of unknown ages past.

The stage went on to Florence. I wandered amid the tangled brush, over ruined heaps of silent clay, that once was vocal with the voice of man, now desolate, silent and alone.

On the north side of these grounds are dry basins and reservoirs with a canal or ditch leading to the Gila River, twenty miles north, wide and deep enough to carry water to water all the plain, and the grading is so perfect that it could not be improved by our most skillful engineers of modern times. It is an unsolved mystery why so much broken pottery is scattered all over and about these ruins. It is painted and striped in geometrical lines, representing much art, and some of it of a fine texture, translucent, representing porcelain. The city was all built of concrete earth, and the massive mounds of debris show that some were very large. A portion of three only yet remain standing. I gave my attention to the principal one which stands directly square with the four cardinal points of the compass. It is 63 long, 45 wide, and 40 feet high, with walls five feet in thickness, plainly representing four stories.

The two corners facing the east have fallen down, and measuring the ridge of debris indicate that they were towers 163 feet high. The roof has all fallen in, and how much of the top walls, can only be judged from the immense quantity of debris inside. The floors have also all fallen down, and nothing now remains but the bare walls, and the partition walls inside. The outside walls were laid in stratas of three feet at a time, and then left to dry, as is still visible by a straight mark or line extending across the building from corner to corner. The inside walls are made smooth, with a hard finish, and as even and perpendicular as our best mechanics could do at the present day.

On the east end are two openings one on the first, and another on the second story, two feet wide and four high, the sides being made smooth as all the openings are, and nothing on the side or bottom to indicate a frame, yet over the top of all these, were poles placed across to support the clay above, which are now all gone, yet the prints remain. On the north side are openings of the same character through one of which I entered, in the west end. On the second story is a circular opening two feet in diameter, very smooth. The south wall has no openings, and stands firm 40 feet high. The interior is walled off into five rooms. On the east end is a wall extending across from the north to the south side, making a hall 10 feet wide and 45 feet long. On the west end is another hall of the same dimension, the body portion is divided into three apartments by two walls extending from the east cross wall, to the west wall, of the same character, making the three rooms 33 by 21 feet each. The thickness of the walls are included in these measurements. From the central north hall, to the middle hall, on the first floor, are openings 15 inches high, and 18 inches long. In the next story above are two openings of the same character as those before mentioned, that open outside. Over all of these were three tier of sticks laid, now all gone. On the upper stories, from room to room, are 14 circular openings a foot in diameter, made very smooth. The floors were made by laying poles four inches in diameter from wall to wall a little distance apart, the ends embedded in the mortar. Across these, at right angles were another tier of smaller poles or sticks 1¼ inches in diameter, with the ends swallow-tailed, and pushed into the clay. The niches in the wall from which they have been displaced presents a smooth surface as though cut with a sharp tool, although not a vestige of the wood could I find to demonstrate the fact. The ends of the poles were universally oval as if cut with a dull tool, which the cavities in the wall show, the wood being pulled out, yet a few bits remain in the walls on the second and third stories to which I climbed by means of a rude zig zag stick, and split off a few bits with my knife. The third covering for the foundation of the floors was a layer of tuiles, the size of a pipe stem, and over all of these was spread a mass of concrete dirt a foot in thickness, as the lines on the wall plainly indicate. Nothing in or about the building shows what means they had of ascending from one story to the other, neither can it be seen how they held the clay in position until it became hardened. It was handled with the naked hand and punched together by means of a round stick, as the prints of both still remain in the hardened clay. Seeing these finger points in the centre of the wall where a portion had been broken off, I laid my hand in it and what thoughts came over me. Where now the hand that made the finger prints my fingers fill? Long, long departed, and age on age has rolled away—blotted from the face of the globe—lost to history—forever, and forever, unknown.

Having spent the day alone in this solitude I returned with the stage to the station at three P. M.

Wednesday morning October 17th at three A. M., I started on again, and a run of 63 miles brought us [to Tucson to breakfast, 987 miles from San Francisco.

Tucson is the second oldest town in the United States, settled by the Jesuit Fathers in 1650, whose mission was to save the souls of the Papago Indians. Tucson, is situated in the Santa Cruz Valley, which contains 3,000 acres of rich fertile land if irrigated. The great highway from Mexico to Arizona has crossed this valley, nearly 300 years. I visited the older portion of the town, and could not dispute history in reference to its age. I walked down into the bed of the river, which is wide and deep enough for vessels to pass through, yet there was not a drop of water in it. Its banks are thickly studded with the old adobe huts, and shanties of mud ; still the abode of human beings, whose sombre appearance added darkness to the scene, while the unnumbered dogs set up such an unearthly howl, I was glad to retire to the cars again. This is a specimen of former Mexican enterprise.

With the advent of the railroad a new era burst upon them. Extensive ware-houses were built, and many of the Government offices are located there. It is also the great shipping point to the mines a hundred miles each way. It has a population of 8,000, Mexicans, Spaniards, Indians, English, and Americans. Drunkenness and carrying weapons are punishable as a crime. The Papagoes, suffer their hair to be cut straight across their shoulders. The Mexicans are as black as the Indians. Pantano is another shipping point, but is merely a collection of adobe huts. A short distance from Pantano we reached a narrow vale where grass and running water were seen, being the first noticed since leaving the Colorado River, 280 miles west. Some rock cutting had also been done, the first to break the monotony of the extensive desert. From Pantano it is 18 miles to Benson, at the junction of the Sonora railroad that runs south to the Gulf of California. It is a stirring place built with wood houses showing enterprise, and is the great shipping point for the surrounding mines, including the great Tombstone mine, 20 miles away. Previous to this, adobe huts, with the word store, has been the most enterprising objects seen, and even the old portion of the town of Benson, along the river, is merely a collection of mud huts, promiscuously thrown in together, where the old Mexicans live a miserable, dirty life, in their dark abodes. At Dragoon Summit, 20 miles from Benson, the desert is virtually left behind, and smooth, grassy prairie is spread out before us, with high, naked mountains on each side.

Cachise, chief of the Apache Indians, made his headquarters in these mountains during the 12 years of his cruel bloodshed.

While passing across this expansive prairie we ran directly on to the bed of a dry lake some miles in extent. The bottom is entirely smooth and covered with an alkaline substance that resembles water in the distance, and is called mirage, which phenomenon has led so many weary travelers astray on the desert.

Wilcox is situated in the centre of the prairie, 50 miles each way, and 1,064 miles from San Francisco. This also is another great shipping point to and from the mines.

Passing across these grassy plains, I noticed large herds of stock and sheep, with fleet little antelopes feeding among them, which on our approach soon vanished from sight. Passing on 24 miles from Wilcox we arrived at Bowie for dinner, which is another great shipping point. Long trains of six mule teams were coming in from the mines with ores, to load back with supplies.

Rolling on 15 miles from Bowie we crossed the line into New Mexico and passed over the bed of another dry lake that extends as far as the eye could reach. Thence on to Lordsbury, a shipping point, to the celebrated Clifton Copper Mines, 80 miles north, and also, for its own mining products.

Being no water on these broad plains, the railroad company dug for it here, and at a depth of 100 feet, struck a ledge of mineral, and followed it 500 feet. Some of the assays run as high as $3,700 per ton. They afterwards sold their claim to a Wall Street Gold and Silver mining company for $2,000,000.

Not a green plant is seen here, and as we pass away we cross the bed of the third dry lake. The prairie now opens out entirely level in one broad ocean of grass, with here and there a cactus rising above the bunch grass around it, and often were seen fleet little antelopes, that like specters in the distance, vanished from sight. Deming is 1,198 miles from San Francisco, at the junction of the Atchison, Topeka and Santa Fe Railroad, with the Southern Pacific.

The road now takes a northeasterly course, 58 miles to Rincon, on the Rio Grande River, 1,256 miles from San Francisco, and strikes a branch that runs directly south about 90 miles to El Paso. Rincon is nearly all adobe, one-story buildings. I stayed here over night, was shown a room adjoining the bar room, which had an arsenal appearance from the guns and cartridges stored therein.

———

Thursday, October 18th, I left Rincon at 5 A. M., took the branch road directly south to El Paso, following the valley of the Rio Grande all the way. Some portions are irrigated but not cultivated, and show a miserable apology for a crop. Little mud cabins from 12 to 16 feet square, are scattered along the river banks, some of which have a small place for light, others have none except the doorway, and yet a second class, that are poorer still, mere kennels, a few plank or sticks forming a tent, and bits of canvas thrown over them, or covered with bark, and broken bits of boards picked out of the river.

A few cotton-wood and willows lined the banks of the stream, and in the distance, to the east, the barren serrated peaks of the mountains reared their naked heads. We arrived at El Paso at 9 A. M., and the first object that met our view was an hundred goats before the station. The Rio Grande was nearly dry, I crossed the pontoon on two or three small boats and found myself in Paso Del Norte, Old Mexico, really a city built of nothing but mud, streets, walls, yards, enclosures and floors, all the same. Inhabited solely by Spanish Mexicans, with whom I could not talk.

The city was built in a manner to ensure defense against Indian attack. On one of the principal streets a block of mud buildings, one story high, with dirt roofs, stretch off at some length, with 18 doors facing the street, but not a pane of glass through the entire length. In the rear is an opening in the wall a foot square with a few slats across it, also a back door opening into an enclosure made of mud 16 feet high.

The water is mostly taken out of the Rio Grande into an irrigating ditch, and carried through the city. It has a muddy, cream colored appearance, yet they all use it. And women were lugging it home in urns on their shoulders. The different trades and merchandise shops have their signs out as in other cities. I noted one read Cassa-de-Jesus Barela Anna-do-barela. The cathedral is a large adobe building with a spire, in which, on ropes hang three bells. The ascent is by spiral steps composed of flatted logs, the outer ends fast in the wall, the central resting on each other. There are but five small windows in the edifice, and they are high up in the walls.

Over the entrance are the words "Haec-est-domus Domine." Inside on the right is the baptismal fount of "Holy Water." The church has no slips or seats, the congregation of course remain standing during service.

The altar is in the farther end of the building, where candles were burning, and before it devout women were on their knees in prayer. Round beams carved in the most ancient style extend from one side to the other overhead, being placed 18 inches apart. On top of these, in a diamond shape, laid close together, is a covering of cane break reeds which forms the ceiling overhead. The supporting posts to the gallery are carved the same as the beams, in diamonds, with a rose in the centre.

This church has stood 308 years. The Paso Del Norte Railroad House, is large and beautiful, the only thing in the city that shows modern enterprise, and sets off in vivid contrast with the surroundings, of mud huts, earth floors, mud chimneys, little open fires, latticed windows, and stupid people. The place has no manufactures or commerce, and a starved market. There is no riding or teaming in the streets, yet a few burro trains are seen loaded with wood, three times the size of their bodies. The chief business seems to be a little mercantile trade; saloons and drinking. A little fruit is raised.

At the close of the day, I left this scene of Mexican enterprise, recrossed the Rio Grande, into Uncle Sam's Dominions, got on board the cars, and followed back the road to Rincon, where it struck the main road again, and continued following up the course of the Rio Grande all night, arriving at Albuquerque.

Friday morning, October 19th.—The old town recedes like darkness at the dawn of day, and the bustle of commerce and business, drive all before them. The soil here appears to be somewhat productive, but they can't stop to till it, perseverence must speed on.

We passed on through Bernalillo and a number of other villages that were mere collections of huts, but turning our eyes to the right, we beheld again the mountains rearing their jagged heads high up to the clouds in desolate nakedness. Many cattle, however, were seen along the river and hundreds of mules.

We stopped at Wallace and took breakfast. The Pueblo Squaws stood around the depot, offering trinkets, pottery, and smoked topaz for sale. They are all Catholics, have a church of their own, live in houses, have much stock, are civilized and well to do, yet they dress in Indian style. The snow clad peaks have burst upon our view in the north once more, while the naked, barren mountains are close at hand. We crossed many dry channels of streams where nothing grew. The Rio Calistard at Las Cerrillos is also dry. We have been for some time toiling up a steep grade to reach Llama Junction, 1,500 miles from San Francisco, and 300 miles from Deming where we arrived at 9 A. M., and at 10.25 took the branch road, 18 miles to Santa Fe, which we reached at 11 A. M., after winding up around the mountains among the scattering shrubs of pine and cedar.

Santa Fe is the oldest recorded town in the United States. Its settlement by the Aztecs extends back into the misty past, where even tradition does not reach it; but its known history commences in 1542, when it was taken by the Spaniards. It had been the headquarters of the Montezumas for hundreds of years before, as the old adobe or mud buildings bore testimony; the relics of which still remain, and are occupied by the same class of the human family, but by marriage and intermarriage with the Spaniards, they have become so blended that the wisest scientist can not tell to which class they belong, and vulgarly are called Greasers. All of this class now wear citizens clothing, are numbered with the Mexicans, who are a very dark race of beings. Santa Fe is the capital of New Mexico, the most important and populous city in the territory. It is a place where the works of antiquity from the mist of ages past, are set side by side in contrast with modern improvement. Learning and refinement, art and science meet heathenism and barbarism face to face, and shake hands.

Every step in the line of progress since 1542 has been indelibly stamped on some object in or around Santa Fe, and can be clearly read to-day in the surrounding scenery. For centuries Santa Fe has been preeminent for learning, culture and wealth. It was a large Pueblo town when the Spaniards entered it, and the Franciscan Fathers came with them as missionaries, to save the souls of the natives. They built a small adobe Catholic church on a mese in the north part of the town, which now lies in ruins. The cemetery close by tells of antiquity, but not of the sleepers who rest below. The first edifice being too small, San Miguels' Church was built in 1582. It was used about 100 years, then partially destroyed in the Aztec rebellion in 1680, of which mention will hereafter be made. It was rebuilt in 1710. It is still standing with the old adobe church yard wall in front. It is preserved and retained intact, for its antiquity. Some ancient pictures are to be seen inside. Admission, 25 cents. At a still later date a third church was built of adobe and rough unhewn stone in which worship is now held.

Fourteen years ago the Roman Catholic Archbishop commenced a new fire proof church, constructing it entirely of beautiful cut stone, which is rapidly approaching completion. It is so large that it completely surrounds and takes in the old edifice; and so high that its arches are keyed overhead, and when they worship in the old tabernacle, their devotions are also offered in the new Archbishop's Cathedral.

I viewed the mouldering ruins of the first, thence on to the glory and magnificence of the last, all in close proximity.

The Governor's house next claimed my attention. I was invited into the Governor's room, and told that the building was used by the Captain General of New Spain, who ruled with despotic power from the days of Pedro de Peratta, in 1600, until the establishment of republican government in 1821. This antiquated palace is built of adobe, and is 300 feet long, 50 wide and one story high, with the wall four feet in thickness, having a broad veranda in front and roofed with dirt, as all the old adobe buildings are. It is nicely plastered inside and well furnished.

Leaving the Governor's Palace, I walked into the Plaza, which is located directly in front. It comprises an acre of ground, tastefully ornamented with trees, walks, lawns and flowers, also containing a beautiful fountain and summer house, near by which stands the Soldiers' Monument of stone, 30 feet high. "To the Heroes of the Federal Army." Close by the side of the old San Miguel Church, stands a beautiful edifice, St. Michaels College, ruled by the Christian Brothers.

Parting with these brothers in friendship, I went to the Convent and Seminary, directed by the Sisters of Lorietta. This is a very beautiful and ornamental edifice, built of cut stone, and is surrounded by a number of acres of irrigated ground that produces very fine fruit. A specimen of which I brought to Kirkland.

The Orphan Asylum is a spacious brick building. The institution is under the direction of the Sisters of Charity. The Bishop's Garden is also a spot of fruit and flowers, irrigated by water from the Santa Fe River, as also are all the gardens and yards in town.

The Academy and University of New Mexico is non sectarian. The former with others institutions of learning bring education within the reach of all.

My footsteps led me to a large cemetery where I noticed the dead forgotten lie, without head-stones or monuments. I also passed over the grounds of old Fort Marcy, now in ruins, and on to the military Headquarters of New Mexico, where soldiers are stationed and the buildings and grounds kept in good shape. Near by stands the Palace Hotel with a capacity for 150 guests. Next the Aztec relics claimed attention, where I noticed many things of ancient days. The mealing stones, a cart 200 years old, pottery, and many articles of ancient Indian origin, some of which represented the former gods worshipped by that race.

From the store I went to the Territorial Exhibition of the resources and minerals of New Mexico. They are exhibited in two buildings, the larger is 60 by 480 feet, for the mineral department; the antiquated articles are shown in the other, where I noticed a stone drill ingeniously worked by a stick and string; a Pueblo Indian plow, which is merely a piece of a small pine shrub, four feet in length, formed like a wedge, with one limb left on for a handle, to this a long, round stick was attached, by which it was formerly drawn by the squaws. It merely rooted up the ground so that they could get in a few hills of corn. I also noticed a Latin Bible, printed in 1506. The ancient scale was a wood balance beam, with a stone in a sack fastened to one end and a wood hook at the other, to hold the commodity to be weighed. The spinning wheel is made like a top, with a long handle, and its whirling motion twisted the thread. A hollow log having holes through the sides served as a corn-stalk press to obtain its sweet juices for syrup. Paintings on buckskin from the old Pecos Church are also shown, representing Santa Barbara; also the old chair used by his excellency, Manuel Alvarez is there.

Passing from here to the mineral department, and viewing the specimens of gold, silver, lead, with other metals, and reading the accounts of the same, it appears as though Arizona alone has metals enough to supply the world.

Santa Fe has very narrow streets, a team standing crosswise would block them up.

Saturday, October 20th.—At 3 P. M., I left my lodgings at P. F. Hurlows' hotel in Santa Fe, and returned to the main line at Llama Junction, and started on again east, with two engines attached to take us up the steep grade and through the pass. The scenery over these mountains is romantic, weird, sublime and beautiful, being more highly prized because when once passed we shall see no more like it, therefore we watched the deep gorges, rock cuttings, winding, twisting and turning of our course up the rugged way, where every moment brought some new object to our view; mountain streams winding their way down into grassy vales that stretch away between the verdant hills, of which we caught one glimpse and they were gone. We reached Glorieta at 7 P. M., and I staid there over night.

The Pueblo Indians were so called because they lived in towns built of mud or unburnt brick instead of wigwams like the savage tribes, and they appear to be descendants of the ancient Egyptians.

At the time of the conquest in 1542, they were supposed to number among the hundreds of thousands. They are now reduced down to 10,000. The ostensible pretence of the early Jesuit Fathers and missionaries was to Christianize the natives, but under their new regime they caused the Pueblos to work in the mines under duress, for the pretended benefit of the church, and the most inhuman cruelties were imposed upon them until 1680, when the Pueblos revolted from the oppressors' yoke. Then a sanguinary and bloody scene of revenge followed. The Spaniards were all killed or driven from the country, their chapels burned down and buildings destroyed.

The Pueblos collected the Church Saints on the Plaza and burnt them, filled up the mines, forbid the use of the Spanish language, and utterly destroyed everything belonging to the Spaniards, except the old Pecos Church, which was built in 1628, and tradition says on the very spot where Montezuma was born. This they held sacred for the reception of Montezuma on his second coming, which they steadfastly believed would occur: that he would come from the east in fire and smoke, with his face shining like the brightness of the sun, enter into his church, and redeem his people. "So great faith was not found in Israel," no, not in the history of the world.

The sacred fire was kept burning day and night, and a watching for his appearing until the present century. Century after century passed away, and they watched and waited still with faith unshaken. Warfare, pestilence, old age and disease gradually lessened their number; yet, still they watched and waited until the last remnant of the tribe disappeared, and the light of their fires went out with their last expiring breath.

The shrine of Montezuma is laid waste, his temple is crumbling back to dust, and that faith "that passeth all understanding" has perished with its believers.

The Pueblo of Pecos, once so populous and devout, now lies forsaken upon a plain, desolate and alone, naught but a shapeless mass of ruins.

Will Montezuma ever come or has he already come from the east, in the spirit of the railroads?

The Pueblo nation held the country 12 years, when the Spaniards returned and reduced them to submission again, and held the country until the establishment of the Mexican Republic in 1821.

Glorieta, Sunday, October 21.—Glorieta has no place for religious worship, and the nearest point where it was ever held, is now the ruins of the old Pecos Church, whither I resolved to go, notwithtanding it was seven miles distant.

I walked six miles on the railroad track; then looking over the pines I saw the ruins of the old church standing on the open plain beyond. Passing through the timber I reached a rocky bed

E

having small round cavities on its surface like mortars for pounding corn. The Pueblo, or village, was built on a table land of a few acres, rising slightly above the surrounding plain.

A rude stone wall, mostly fallen except the gateway, surrounded the crest of this plateau. Inside the wall and encircling around the same, are the chaotic ruins of their once rude dwellings, forming a hollow in the centre, in which are two basins in a round form fifty feet in diameter, with a chimney arising from one.

The dwellings were built of broken fragments of stone laid in mud in the rudest style. Their size was from eight to twenty feet long and eight feet wide, and some of them two stories high, with six feet walls each. The entrance to the lower story was so small that a person could not get in without laying down and crawling in. Possibly these were cellars. The roofs have all fallen in save one. The floors were built by laying split sticks from wall to wall, covered with reeds and a foot of dirt on top. They were roofed in the same way.

I found one of their mills, but could not bring it. I noticed outside the wall, on the side of the hill, piles of ashes, where fires long had burned, and nearly every rock around the elevation shows signs of fire being kindled by it. On one side I found little ovens three feet long, two feet wide, and three feet deep, all fallen in. Whether for baking, reducing ore or for pottery, does not appear. Broken pottery is scattered all over. On the north side of the hill I also noticed a sepulchre unearthed, composed of mortar or cement a foot in thickness, and as large as a wine tierce. It was broken down and robbed, and the bones thrown out to bleach on the sand. No other marks of burial were seen. The ruins of the old Pecos Church stand on the eastern portion of the grounds. This antiquated edifice was built in 1628, of unburnt brick, the straw in which is still visible. Its size is 150 by 60 feet on the ground, with walls six feet thick; the front has fallen down, the back and side walls are still standing about forty feet high. There are a few openings for light, but nothing to show that windows, doors, or even floors were ever used.

Some portions of timber still remaining in the walls show that ancient style of carving peculiar to Catholic churches. While standing alone inside in solemn thought, I could but ask myself the question, where now the busy crowd that once assembled to worship here? A low spirit voice replied, "They've gone to rest, where you soon must go." I bent the knee before that God who once was worshiped there, then turned my back upon the lonely scene, and walked away leaving all behind.

Monday, October 22d.—At 2.30 A. M., I left Glorieta, and passed on to Las Vegas, 65 miles from Lama. This is quite a commercial town in the centre of a mining district, with a population of 9,000. Six miles north of Las Vegas, on a branch road, are located the celebrated Las Vegas Hot Springs, flowing from the foot of the mountain on the banks of the Gallinas River, immediately after it leaves the canon in the Spanish range of mountains. At this point nature has formed a plateau of thirty acres with high towering mountains all around it, except where the Gallinas River enters and leaves the plateau.

There are many of these springs, sixteen of which have been nicely walled up with cut stones. Their temperature ranges from 71° to 136° F.

Little had been done to improve these springs until 1879, when a bath-house was built, 200 feet long, 42 feet wide, and two stories high, composed of red granite, and capable of administering 500 baths daily. A fine hotel was also erected at the same time and of the same material. Red, white and gray granite are found in the same quarry and rest side by side.

In 1881, the Atchison, Topeka and Santa Fe Railroad Company purchased the entire property, erected a branch road to the springs, and built at the same time a large public house called the Montezuma, with a capacity for 300 guests. Rates, three to four dollars per day. The water supply of the town comes from a lake basin three and a half miles away.

The baths are of every variety, such as medicated, electric, vapor, shampoon, douche, ring-baths, spray, shower and mud baths. This last is an unheard of bath at any other place on the globe, yet, it is said to be the most efficatious of them all, and is administered in a separate building, erected for that purpose alone. When I came near the door a gentleman invited me in and explained the mode of procedure. The springs make their appearance some rods from the stream. The hot water has run through the mud for untold ages. The result is, the soil has absorbed the chemical properties of the water, and the application of it to the body effects the cure. The mud is about six feet deep, and resembles lard and lampblack mixed together. It is shoveled up and reduced in a bath tub to the thickness of cream, after which the patient is plunged in and remains as long as he choose, then is washed off with clear water, and appears in his native color, a white man again.

I was shown around a beautiful Club House, and told that the inhabitants there all gambled.

The surroundings of the town are wild; perpendicular walls rise up beside the railroad track, and lofty blades shoot up from their summits. Before leaving I amused myself by testing the heat of the water from nature's fountain. Being provided with the necessary apparatus, I put my tea to drawing, it steaped very nicely, and the other articles were made palatable in a short time. Next I gave my attention to the natives of the vicinity. Walking down the track a mile, three Mexican adobe towns were in sight, standing on the open plain a little back from the river. Round about these dwellings and towns not a tree, shrub, plant, vine or green blade of any kind could be seen, nothing visible about them but utter nakedness. How do those people live?

I was walking in a town of Penitents, therefore I noticed them the more. The town contains about fifty houses, nestling under the brow of a hill, and are variously constructed. Some are laid up with rough bits of stone placed in mud, poles put closely together over the top, and covered with mud. Others are built by setting four crotches in the ground with poles laid in them, and other poles standing perpendicular, close together all around, and plastered up with mud; then roofed the same as the others. A third kind are built of round poles laid in cob house form, plastered with mud and roofed the same. A few of the better class are built of adobe, yet dirt forms the roofs of all, and native earth their floors. They have but one small, low doorway for entrance. Some have one pane of glass for light, but more have none. Inside is a little rude bunk. Their few dishes and clothing are in a box, hang on the wall, or lie on the ground. A small fire-place is in one corner with a little mud chimney through the roof. Their ovens are of clay, built outside, and are the most healthy looking things about them.

They are very dark complexion, wearing long, black hair, and hats with broad brims, having one or two braided bands encircling them, and when they travel on horseback, they are always seen to go on a canter. No business of any kind is done in the town except what is done at one or two saloons. Corn meal and water unleavened and baked, called Tortier Cake, forms their bread, and red-pepper with meat and vegetables their luxury.

These penitents are seceding Catholics, believing in self-persecution for their sins, and during Easter, called Passion Week, intense religious enthusiasm exists.

On top of the mountain is a large cross where the leader of their sect was buried; he not being considered orthodox, was not permitted to be buried on Holy Ground. They crawl up to it, dragging their naked persons over the rocks and lashing each other with rattail thorny cactus, until their bodies are covered with blood. So much for their religious faith. It is said that these towns are lordships, and belong to one man, who owns flocks and herds, and mines, making the people virtually slaves, or wholly dependent on his will. Such towns are called Peons. The inhabitants are ignorant, superstitious and always in debt to their lords and not suffered to depart as long as they are in debt, which appears to be always the case.

The native production are Pinyons, a small burr nut from the Pinyon Pine tree, and cactus, from which wine of a poor quality is sometimes made. I left the Springs and came down to the main line at Las Vegas at 7 P. M., and retired—363 miles from Denning, and 785 miles from Kansas City.

Tuesday, the 23d, at 3.45 A. M., we rolled directly out on to a vast, expansive, grassy plain, reaching Wagon Mound at daylight, and passing the little adobe town of Springer at sunrise, where we saw large herds of cattle scattered over the plains. On the left, in the distance, the lofty Rockies rear their mighty heads, white with snow.

Our early transit over the plains started up two droves of ante-lopes, that fled for life. We stopped at Raton for breakfast, after which two powerful engines were attached to the train and puffed and tugged us up to the pass, directly into the bowels of the mountains. A screech of the whistle signaled good-bye to the rear engine, and we were at once plunged into the Raton Tunnel, and entered Colorado on a down grade, and passed 786 feet in darkness, then emerged into daylight on the other side, to see far down below our feet the vast, expanded plain spread out before us as far as the eye could reach. The down grade is very steep, but by twisting, winding and turning we at length reached the plain below to find only a few adobe huts, mud plastered cabins, and dug-outs in the side-hill at a place called Starkville, where there are immense mines of coal, lying under the mountains on the left, where we passed around a high, castle rock, and stopped and took dinner at Trinidad, situated at the foot of another high peak over-looking the town. The valley widens out with a rich soil, six feet deep covered with sage bush, and producing well where irrigated. From Trinidad we launched directly out into that vast ocean of grassy prairie so lately viewed from the top of the mountain behind. The sage bush now disappears, and to it, good-bye—we have inhaled its odors long enough. So to, those dingy, mudbuilt Mexican towns, are left behind.

And to the rugged massive towering cliffs, deep gorged through mountains high, that move the heart and thrill the nerves, inspiring awe for Him who gave them form, to all, farewell! farewell!

Herds of cattle and flocks of sheep are now in order, and are scattered far and near upon the open plain; but no barns or sheds are seen to shelter them.

Swiftly rolling on across the plains, we at length reached La Junta, on the Arkansas River at the junction of the Denver and Rio Grande Railroad, with the Atchinson, Topeka, and Santa Fe Railroad. Here we turned our course directly east, following the river till 10 P. M., when we crossed the line into Kan-sas, still continuing on the river banks all night, brought us to Nickerson, Wednesday morning, October 24. This is a smart little town, but now, is flooded with rain, the first I have seen for six weeks. Thus far the State is little else than a grassy plain, in its native wildness.

We still continued down the water course to Halsted where it turned at right angle to the south and left us to strike off east on this boundless expanse of plain, which now begins to show signs of cultivation.

Stacks of hay appear and fall sown wheat is seen on the ground. We stopped at Newtown for breakfast, where peaches, quinces, and other fruits grow, yet corn and wheat are the principal products of the land, while nature has richly provided them with an extensive quarry of red sandstone for buildings, which extends to Crawford.

The remaining 150 miles to Kansas City is level, with a rich productive soil, and well cultivated as the stacks of hay and grain attest, being no barns. Coal is found in abundance, the shipments amounting to $6,000,000 annually.

I arrived at Topeka, Kansas, 2.30 P. M. This is a large city of 24,000 inhabitants, regularly laid out, yet the streets are not paved, and in a wet time are intolerable. The town embraces nine square miles of surface, and has the shops where all the cars used on the Atchinson, Topeka and Santa Fe Railroad are made; it also contains many fine buidings, and all the societies and institutions of the day. The State House is being constructed after the pattern of the Capitol at Washington.

An iron bridge 900 feet long connects the two parts of the city, spanning the Kansas River, which is not navigable. Some parks are laid out, and on one is a Prairie Dog Town. These little pets resemble the dog and squirrel, have short legs, and short tails, but when they eat they sit on their hind feet and hold their food in their fore paws. They are very tame and came up and smelt of our fingers for food, but refused to be handled.

On the approach of a dog they all dodge back into their burrows, but soon come to the light again, and peek out, and if the adversary is gone, they are out at once and seen on the lawn, barking, feeding and at play.

The soil on these expanded plains is deep and rich, producing large crops when cultivated. Apples are very fine and high colored. Various kinds of sweet potatoes are produced, as well as all the common vegetables, cereals and grains. Soft coal is abundant at $4 per ton.

Thursday, October 25, at four in the afternoon, I pursued my journey, reaching Kansas City at eight in the evening, and took rooms at the United States Hotel. This is one of the largest cities of the west, with a population of 70,000, comprising an upper and lower town. The lower town is a great railroad centre, and the emporium of the city.

This portion is down on the river bottoms, and in a wet time is one perfect sea of slop and mud. The stock yards were filled with stock and swine unnumbered, and the manufactures of wagons and agricultural implements are immense. The iron structure across the Kansas River is 600 feet long, having no draw. A short distance below the bridge the waters of the Kansas River unite with those of the Missouri. A cable road connects the upper and lower town. The upper town is regularly laid out, containing many fine buildings, chiefly brick, manufactured on the ground, and ready for use as soon as moulded and baked. An immense army are employed in the business cutting down the banks 30 or 40 feet, and utilizing the material for brick.

They work with astonishing alacrity. Twelve men in 10 hours, will turn out from raw material 21,400 brick. The upper streets of the city are being improved by laying concrete crushed stone a foot thick over them, covering the same with sand, on which cedar blocks seven inches in length are closely set, the crevices being filled with fine gravel and sand.

Before leaving the city I ascended the high bluffs that rise abruptly from the Missouri River, and my eyes wandered up and down this mighty and majestic stream.

It slowly curls its way along in grand sublimity, yet it has no transparent beauty, for its waters are always sluggish and of a roily cream color. The railroad bridge that crosses the river at this point is built of iron, 14,000 feet long, and the portion that crosses the bed of the stream comprises seven spans, and cost one and a half million dollars. Strange as it may appear to a Yankee, this river is the recipient of all the manure and refuse of the city.

Kansas City, the eastern terminal of the Atchison, Topeka and Santa Fe Railroad, is 2,259 miles east from San Francisco, and on the west line of the State of Missouri.

At 6.20 P. M. I took a seat in a Palace Reclining Chair Car, on the Alton and Chicago Railroad and started east to cross the State of Missouri. These cars are said to be the finest in the world. One pane of glass comprises each window, and the intermediate spaces are set with mirrors, forming a glass palace. The reclining chairs are upholstered in the richest style, and can be adjusted to suit the convenience of the occupant. The best of meals are also served on board at 75 cents.

The rich productiveness and fertility of the soil of Missouri, has so long been known, that I reclined in one of the chairs to rest and passed it by, and on the morning of Saturday, October 27th, I arrived in St. Louis.

St. Louis is one of the most populous cities of the west, containing 360,000 inhabitants. A great railroad center; ten lines come in to the Union Depot. The street crossings are all bridged over head. It has a fine State House, Court House and Jail, and many fine and lofty buildings, but generally aside from its parks, it presents a scene of business bustle and confusion. The buildings are brick and the smoke, ashes and dust, that have settled upon them give to the whole a dingy appearance; and the streets being low, they are flooded with mud.

I took the street cars to the Zoological Gardens five miles distant, through densely populated, narrow, muddy streets; but nothing of interest presented itself. Then I turned my attention to the massive iron railroad bridge that crosses the Mississippi River. It is a collossal work, and astonishing to behold how man can overcome apparent insurmountable difficulties. The bridge is sufficiently high for all the river crafts to pass under it; and the foundations are said to rest 90 feet below high water mark.

The iron network of which the three broad arches are composed, that span the water surface, is truly immense. It is also a double bridge, street cars, and street travel on top, and railroad cars under. Including the approaches I should consider it to be a mile in length. I crossed it twice by daylight on the cars, and walked out to the centre of it on foot, and looked down on that Mighty Mother of waters of North America.

The banks of the river are so high that as soon as the cars leave the approaches they at once plunge into a tunnel, and pass for a mile and a quarter directly under the very heart of the city, making an egress at the Union Depot.

The redeeming qualities and beauty of St. Louis, are more vividly manifest in the beauty and neatness of her parks. I took a street car and passed out five miles in an opposite direction from the other route, but through the same class of muddy streets, until I arrived at the City Park, containing 275 acres. I there found the Elysian Fields. Marble columns shot up on each side the gateway bearing lion-like statuary on top, while others bore creatures imaginary. Passing through I found the park house a very fine building and some offices. The grounds are laid out in the most tasty style with walks, lawns and drives. The drives run in every imaginary direction over the grounds, and are composed of white stone, crushed very fine, looking quite neat and beautiful. Streams of water pass through the grounds, skirted with weeping willows. A number of exquisite and substantial summer houses are scattered about the lawn supporting bugle honey suckle, and various clambering vines. A crystal fountain of water adorns the central portion. Humboldt's Statue stands on a high pedestal by the side of the main drive; and various others are seen about the lawns. Evergreen trees and shrubs are scattered here and there all over, representing every conceivable form and shape of training. Pines, cedars, firs, and many foreign trees I could not name; one bearing a round leaf six feet in circumference having no branches, merely a single stem. An evergreen hedge encloses the whole, and Osage oranges hung on the trees and lay on the ground about it. At the upper end of the park I entered the conservatory and found a rare collection of tropical, and semi-tropical plants and flowers. I left this beautiful scene, passing out at the upper gateway into the open country, and looked away in the distance over a land of corn, but not of wine. I next entered the private grounds and gardens of the great land holder, Henry Shaw. It comprises 40 acres, surrounded by a high stone wall. It is all laid out in plats with drives; and the intermediate space is set with roses and flowers of endless variety. A summer house occupies the centre, and walks diverge from it in all directions through the flowery lawns. The conservatory is quite extensive, containing many tropical plants; among which I noticed Pandurus ve dilus, a specie of palm, and the Philadendron pertusum, also the Monstera Delicosa; all new varieties to me. Near the pallatial residence is a small gothic structure on which I read, "O Lord, how manifold thy works—in wisdom hast Thou made them all." St. Louis is 2,645 miles east of San Francisco.

At 6.55 P. M., I took the cars again, passed through the tunnel under the city coming out at the bridge, and crossed over the Mississippi River to East St. Louis, in the State of Illinois; then pursuing my journey, still eastward on the Indianapolis and St. Louis Railroad across the State of Illinois, into the State of Indiana, arriving at Indianapolis to breakfast at the National Hotel, Sunday morning, Oct. 28th, 1883, 2,908 miles from San Francisco.

Although it had rained three days, yet I found Indianapolis a clean city, regular in form, with well paved streets and fine flag walks, a very large commercial city containing 100,000 inhabitants.

The buildings are large, commodious and fine; many being built of iron and stone, are quite imposing. The State has caught the spirit of the age, and is building a State Capitol of cut stone, on which three years' labor has been spent, and will require five more to finish it up. It comprises an entire block. Catalpa, soft maple and elm trees, adorn their streets and parks. In churches, for number and beauty, Brooklyn here finds a rival. I give them as they appear on the city register:

Methodist Episcopal, 23; Presbyterian, 14; Baptist, 13; Catholic, 7; Christian, 6; Lutheran, 6; Episcopal, 5; German Reformed, 3; Congregational, 2; Hebrew, 2; Episcopal Reformed, 1; Evangelical Association, 1; Friends, 2; Methodist Protestant, 1; Swedenborgian, 1; United Brethren, 1, and the United Presbyterian, 1; being 88 in all.

At 10.30 the doors being open, I was given a seat in Grace Church. Text, John 12, 32d. Preaching good and music fine. After service the Methodist brethren extended to me the hand of fellowship, and invited me to call again. I realized that God dwelt in the hearts of his people everywhere.

Returning past the door of the Third Presbyterian Church, fine music within caused me to linger, and I was seated there. The first question to the class was, which is the greatest commandment of all? Would men but practice the sentiment, as readily as the interrogation was answered, earth would be a terrestial paradise.

Indianapolis has also many humane institutions. The Asylum for the Blind is a large, imposing cut-stone edifice, in the center of a square set with beautiful trees, shrubs and flowers, the happy inmates can never see, although they walk among them, in threes and fives, clasped arm in arm, singing cheerfully.

The fine structures, long, broad, straight streets embowered in trees, render this place one of the loveliest cities of the west, yet I could not tarry long.

Monday, October 29th, at 4 A. M., I moved forward again on the Cincinnati and Indianapolis Railroad, over a beautiful rich country of level land, without a hill, dale, or mountain to break the monotony of the scene, with naught but one continuous stretching on, on, of agricultural producing soil. Corn, wheat, cereals, hay, cattle, sheep, and hogs, are all important articles of commerce. About 10 A. M., at Union City, we passed the State line into Ohio, where the soil is no less fertile, but timber abounds, which reminded me of my childhood days, especially when passing the many log cabins scattered along the way.

The Ohio farmer lays out little for gaudy show. His chief pride and glory is in well tilled lands, enclosed with strong, high fences, bountiful crops, safely stored, and flocks and herds of various kinds scattered over his field, all kept securely under his own guardian care.

In the afternoon we passed Galion, a fine town of 6,000 inhabitants and a railroad centre, arriving at Cleveland, on Lake Erie, at 5 P. M., 3,191 miles from San Francisco, and took rooms at the Lake Shore House. The first thing that attracted my attention was the electric lights that illuminate the city. There are four in number, each one displaying eight lights in a circle, resting on top of a staff of boiler iron, the lower end of which rest again on a massive flag-stone twenty feet below the surface of the earth. They then rise from the surface into the air respectively as follows: The first, 200 feet; second, 240; third, 250, and the fourth, 260 feet, making the darkest night brilliant as the rising day.

This city has many natural advantages that add much to its beauty and scenery. Situated as it is on the banks of the lake, whose restless waters are ever pure and transparent to gaze upon, inspiring the soul with awe and reverence. Its elevated position makes it arid and healthful, while the crystal streams of water flowing through its suburbs add much to its romantic beauty.

The city is very handsomely built, with broad, well paved streets and flag walks, all neat and clean, beautified by airy grounds, lawns, and parks, set with lovely flowers, while the whole is embowered with overshadowing trees. Superior street is the great business thoroughfare of the city. On this street are two fine parks, set with trees and flowers. One of these contains a fountain near which stands a massive stone monument to the memory of the hero of Lake Erie, Commodore Oliver Hazard Perry, his statue being represented as the crowning figure. On the opposite side of the park is a speaker's stand, composed of finely-cut stone, well elevated and spacious enough on top to seat one hundred dignitaries, having also the means of gas and awnings. Encircling these grounds are the finest buildings in the city.

The postoffice comprises an entire block, being built of cut stone, doing honor to the nation. The Forest City House, Court House, and Theatre are large imposing structures of cut stone, and the jail well represents the purpose for which it was built. Although these buildings express grandeur, strength and durability, yet the stone of which they are composed shows a dinginess, and they can not be said to be extremely beautiful.

Tuesday, October 30th, I walked to the shore of the lake. All the railroad lines follow close by the water's edge. The land rises back from this to the table lands on which the city stands 200 feet above. Along the crest are located beautiful residences. The sloping portion in front down to the railroad lines is one continuous park for miles, set with shrubs, plants and flowers, interspersed with lawns, through which walks and drives meander round, and limpid streams with cascades fair add still more loveliness to the scene.

At 8 A. M. I took the street car for Lake View Cemetery, six miles distant, on the outskirts of the city. The line of travel represented a park appearance all the way, on which we passed the residence of Mrs. Garfield, a fine mansion built of pressed brick. On the opposite side of the street are a fine park and conservatory. After some changes we arrived at the ground, and a broad field of 300 acres comprising the cemetery, was spread out before us, containing hills, vales, lawns, streams of water, cascades, fountains, ponds with swan and wild flowls floating on them; also many trees, shrubs, plants, vines and flowers, besides the many tombs, costly and magnificent monuments which sadly tell of friends who heedeth not, but calmly sleep below.

The first attraction on entering the ground was to visit the tomb where temporarily rest the remains of President Garfield.

Passing up a vale by many tombs I at length came to Scofield's new tomb, a fine and beautiful structure. The relief soldiers came at 10 A. M., went through the manual of arms and tactics, discharged the former guard, there being 12 soldiers in all, fully armed, who march to and fro before the sepulchre night and day.

The outer door being opened displayed a casket inside in which the remains of our beloved President rest, with a handful of wheat lying by its side, and a wreath of the same resting on the lid, while palms of victory encircle it round, and a wreath of precious flowers adorns the front.

On the upper portion of the grounds, in a glass house is the car on which he was brought to the cemetry, with all its sable adornments on it, of crape, palls, plumes, and everlastings, canopied with the national flag, stars and stripes.

On the highest portion of the ground, overlooking the lake in its ever restless motion, is being graded and prepared a site for the foundation of the Garfield monument. Among the many fine granite statues on those grounds, that of Rebecca L., wife of Joseph II. Wade, stands forth the most conspicuous, it rests on a base 10 feet square, 2 1-2 feet in thickness. The second base, die and cap, add about 14 feet to the height, on this stands a spire rising 40 or 50 feet in the air, crowned by an angelic figure, standing erect, with the right arm stretched upwards, and finger pointing to Heaven.

Leaving the mansions of the dead, I returned to the city and crossed the viaduct over the Caughoga River and valley. This bridge is a mile in length, and 80 feet high, resting on massive stone arches all the way.

The chimneys from the immense manufactures below, send up a cloud of smoke that darkens the air. The old town on the west side has few charms, yet I noticed one fine park, and a rustic fountain. From here I repaired to the Lake Shore House for the night.

——

Wednesday morning, October 31st, I moved on again eastward on the Lake Shore road, by the side of the beautiful lake. On reaching Ashtabula, the train slowly moved across the gorge, down into which I looked, where once that fatal accident occurred, and the blood chilled in my veins, as fancy brought to my ears the moans and groans of the scorched and dying, still pleading in anguish from the ground. A little farther along we passed Erie in Pennsylvania, situated on the lake, a large business town of 35,000 inhabitants, and also Dunkirk with a population of 9,000, arriving at Buffalo in the afternoon, 3,374 miles from the Pacific Coast.

The business transactions of Buffalo are so well understood that it would be superfluous even to mention them, therefore, I passed on 23 miles farther to Niagara Falls and rested for the night at a very quiet Temperance House.

——

Thursday, November 1st, I paid my entrance fee at the Goat Island Gate, 50 cents, and walked out upon the iron bridge which is 360 feet long, and spans the American Channel just above the falls. From this bridge I had a commanding view of the rapids on the American side. Chained as by magic to the spot, I watched the ever dashing, constant changing, madly rushing foaming waves, in their chaotic confusion, until they passed beneath my feet, and plunged headlong into the awful gulf below.

Crossing this bridge I reached Bath Island which is the largest of a group of 15 that lie in the American Channel, directly at the head of the falls.

The paper mill on this island is the largest in the State. A few feet distant is a small island called " Lovers' Retreat.". Passing over a short iron bridge I stood on Goat Island. The island is owned by the Porter family, who have held it since 1818. It contains sixty-one acres of land in all its primeval beauty and loveliness—a Sylvan bower, a native wooded isle, romantic as it was when nature's plastic hand first gave it form. It divides the river into two parts, causing the two falls. A carriage-road encircles the island.

Turning to the right and following around beneath the forest trees, one-fourth of a mile down the rapids, I came to the Hog's Back, the extreme point of the island, some feet above the flowing current. Passing down to the water's edge and crossing a short bridge, I reached Luna Island, which lies on the brink of the precipice, separating a portion of water from the main stream called the Center Fall, and forming the cave of the winds below.

From Luna Island Mr. Addington and Miss Annetta Deforest passed over the falls and were lost.

Retracing to the main island, I looked back under the precipice of Luna Island, and saw three Giant Profiles, of rock formation. A few steps brought me to the Cave of the Wind's Dressing-rooms, where a fee of one dollar is charged to enter this cave with a guide. I passed down the spiral way of the Biddle stairs, per-pendicular eighty feet, and reached the broken, fallen fragments of rock, which are still 105 feet from the surface of the water below, into which Sam Patch made his famous leap in 1829.

From the foot of Biddle's Stairs I turned towards the Cave of the Wind, through which I once passed five times in one morning. The projecting rocks above, from which the water falls, form the cave, and the compression of the atmosphere causes the dashing and whirling of the spray, like a most violent thunder storm.

From the Biddle Stairs to the Canada Fall the way has been obstructed by slides and fallen portions of rock, and now no path leads that way, yet still I picked along, over, under and around the fallen masses, and across steep, shelly points, until I approached to the very foot of the great cataract, and could look up its entire height and behold its grandeur.

Although my brow was laved with spray and my clothes drenched with the fallen water, yet the sight well repaid the toil. Turning back and ascending the stairs, I walked along the brink of the precipice to the top of the fall above, directly over where I had so lately been below.

Chained here in awful silence; I viewed the
Inspiring scene: my words can ne'er express
Awakened thought, and feeling deep, that stirred
Mine inmost soul. Steadfastly gazing on
The scene sublime; and yet how terrible!
The roaring waters speak Jehovah's name.
The maddened flood, rolling its waters down;
Surging and foaming as it rushes on
In wrathful fury.

Wave after wave behind;
In quick succession press the waves before,
And drive them on until they reach the brink,
Then headlong plunge into the gulf beneath.
Reluctant still to go, the struggling spray
Attempts to rise, then melting down to tears,
Falls back upon itself, and sinks again.
Still o'er those restless, troubled waves below;
The Bow of Promise shines, for God is there.

Turning from this thrilling scene and walking up the bank a little way, I came to the Three Sister Island, which I found my way to by means of three iron bridges, and from the most distant one I took my last view of the rapids.

Returning to the main island and advancing a little farther, I arrived at the head of Goat Island that divides the river. From this point, looking up the river, can be seen Navy Island, from which, on the 29th of December, 1837, the ill-fated Caroline was cut loose from her moorings, set on flames and sent over the falls. " The head of Goat Island is noted in history as being the place where the Hermit Francis Abbott once lived. He was carried over the falls June 10th, 1841.

Recrossing the bridge to the main land, and a faw steps down brought me to Prospect Park, where a gate fee of 25 cents is received. From the plateau to the water's edge below is an inclined railway, fare down 25 cents. From here visitors can go behind the falling sheet under the shadow of the rock for one dollar.

Twenty-five cents more is demanded to be ferried across the channel, over water 192 feet deep to the Canada shore where we find a carriage in waiting to convey guests to the Clifton House to dinner, after which the museum must be visited, then being provided with water-proof dresses and a guide for which one dollar more is paid, to pass under Table Rock and Horse-shoe Fall.

When emerging from this watery cavern and changing rig, we find a carriage in waiting to convey us to the Burning Springs a mile up the river. Fare 50 cents, entrance 50 cents added.

Near this Burning Spring July 5th, 1814, the battle of Chippewa was fought, and ten days later, one and a half miles from the falls, was fought the great battle of the war of 1814, at Lundy's Lane. A high tower or observatory is located at this place, and the cost to and from is the same as to the Burning Spring.

Two miles below, on the Canada side, is located an inclined elevator to enable visitors to descend to the Whirlpool Rapids; fare fifty cents, and fifty cents more admits one the Whirlpool itself.

One of the most daring exploits ever performed by man transpired at the Rapids June 6th, 1861, when the adventurous Robinson and two others rode safely through on the Maid of the Mist.

There are three bridges across this mighty gorge. The oldest is two miles below the falls, a railroad suspension bridge, 822 feet span, 258 feet above water. The new Suspension Bridge is one-quarter of a mile below the falls. It is the longest bridge of the kind in the world; its roadway is 1,300 feet in length, its cables 1,800 feet, and is 190 feet above water. The third is the new Cantilever Bridge for the Canada Southern Railway. Its entire length is 895 feet. The length of cantilevers are 375 and 395 feet, the fixed span 125, and the clear span across the river 500 feet. The stone abutments are 50 feet high, and the steel towers resting on them 130 feet high, and the clear span is 245 feet above the river. This is the only completed bridge of the kind in America, if not in the world. The bridge was being constructed when I was there and appeared the most daring piece of work I ever saw performed. Men suspended on a staging 240 feet in the open air, with a boiling flood 250 feet deep beneath them.

The day having closed I repaired to the cars and was soon on my way to Utica, where I arrived at midnight, and on Friday, November 2d, 1883, I safely arrived at home.

In conclusion, I will merely say, this little volume is bestowed on my friends in its naked self, without preamble or apology, to stand by its own merits, or fall by its demerits, as the case may be, being the first effort of the kind in a lifetime, and peradventure may be the last.

L. D. LUKE,
Kirkland, Oneida County, N. Y.

www.ingramcontent.com/pod-product-compliance
Lightning Source LLC
Chambersburg PA
CBHW030004030726
47499CB00008B/2883